ISBN 978-0-266-87415-7
PIBN 10902734

BULLETIN OF THE
U.S. DEPARTMENT OF AGRICULTURE
No. 22

Contribution from the Bureau of Biological Survey, Henry W. Henshaw.
Chief. September 16, 1913.

GAME LAWS FOR 1913

A SUMMARY OF THE PROVISIONS RELATING TO SEASONS, EXPORT, SALE, LIMITS, AND LICENSES.

By T. S. Palmer, W. F. Bancroft, and Frank L. Earnshaw,
Assistants, Biological Survey.

INTRODUCTION.

SCOPE OF THE BULLETIN.

The present bulletin, containing the fourteenth annual summary of the game laws of the United States and Canada, has been prepared on the same general plan as those issued each year since 1902. It contains a summary of the more important features of the new legislation, a brief synopsis of the new game laws enacted in each State and Province, and a series of tables showing the provisions relating to seasons, export, sale, limits, and licenses. It differs from other publications on the game laws in several important points: (1) Inclusion of a brief but comprehensive review of the measures enacted, (2) arrangement of provisions by subjects instead of by States, and (3) adoption of a uniform statement and order of the various details to facilitate ready comparison of similar provisions in different States. Its chief objects are to present in convenient form the restrictions on hunting which affect the enforcement of the Federal statutes regulating interstate commerce in game and the protection of migratory birds, and to show the trend and general condition of legislation from year to year. Provisions relating to methods of capture, game refuges, enforcement of laws, disposition of fines and fees, and matters of special or local application are omitted. These can be found only by reference to the laws themselves or to the pamphlet editions of the game laws, obtainable in most States from the proper officials.[1]

---

[1] A directory of these officers, with their addresses, is published as Circular No. 94, Biological Survey U. S. Department of Agriculture, 1913.

With the rapidly growing complexity of regulations—Federal, State, and local—in 50 States and Territories, and the constantly increasing number of persons who hunt, the demand for information concerning game laws is spreading. The problem of how to keep the public informed of the numerous yearly changes taxes the ingenuity of officials, and can be solved only by the fullest cooperation on the part of the press, private associations, and individuals.

LEGISLATION IN 1913.

The game legislation of 1913, while large in volume, is not much larger than that of 1911 or 1909, owing to the following causes: Codification bills were enacted in Maine, Oregon, and Vermont; practically all the changes made in Illinois, Montana, New York, Utah, Washington, and Wyoming were embodied in single bills; and all legislation failed in Georgia, daho, Nebraska, New Mexico, South Carolina, and Texas.

Legislative sessions were held in 43 States, 8 Canadian Provinces, and Newfoundland. Numerous bills affecting game were under consideration in nearly every State, and regulations for the protection of migratory game and insectivorous birds in the United States and game in Alaska were promulgated by the Department of Agriculture.

NOVEL OR IMPORTANT PROVISIONS.

Among the various provisions found in the new laws are several novel features directly affecting the hunter or the conditions under which game may be hunted:

Ohio and Pennsylvania now require licensees to wear a badge conspicuously exposed, bearing the number of his hunting license. In order to minimize shooting accidents, Manitoba requires hunters to wear a white coat or sweater and cap, and Saskatchewan insists that those who hunt big game must wear a complete outer suit and cap of white. The latter Province has recently made the penalty for accidentally shooting a person a fine ranging from $500 to $1,000, or imprisonment for six months, and suspension of further license privileges for 10 years. To the present list of six States prohibiting the use of silencers—namely, Maine, New Jersey, North Dakota, Washington, Mississippi, and Louisiana—are now added Minnesota and Wyoming. Connecticut has provided that any hunter who shall injure a fence or let down a bar without replacing it shall forfeit his hunting license and the license privilege for two years. Connecticut, Pennsylvania, and British Columbia require license applicants under 16 years of age to furnish the written consent of parent or guardian. Vermont has a similar restriction for those under 15, and Oregon does not permit children under 14 years old to hunt except on the premises of their parents, relatives, or guardians.

An interesting experiment has been undertaken in Utah, where the game commissioner, with the concurrence of the State board of examiners, is authorized to set aside and maintain a public hunting reserve in the counties of Salt Lake, Davis, and Box Elder.

Numerous States are restocking preserves with elk and other big game. In the effort to protect this game Pennsylvania, Vermont, West Virginia, and Wisconsin have protected elk for a term of years, and in Massachusetts, where a few moose have escaped from the Blue Mountain Forest Reserve into the adjoining woodlands, a perpetual close season for moose has been provided in the hope that this area may eventually be restocked from this nucleus.

REFUGES.

One of the marked features of the legislation of the year was the unusual progress in the establishment of bird and game refuges. By Executive order four national bird reserves have been created, the Aleutian Reservation, containing the entire chain of Aleutian Islands, in Alaska, and the smaller reservations of Walker Lake in Arkansas, Petit Bois Island on the coast of Alabama, and Anaho Island in Pyramid Lake, Nevada, thus bringing the total number of national bird reservations up to 64. During recent months the Niobrara Bird Reservation has also been enlarged and stocked with a herd of buffalo, elk, and deer. An item in the act of March 4, 1913, contains an appropriation for the completion and maintenance of the elk refuge in Wyoming.

No less than 18 State game preserves were created, 14 in the United States and 4 in Manitoba. In Washington the county game commissioners were authorized to create game preserves, not to include more than three townships in a county, and the authorities of Michigan, Ohio, and Vermont were authorized to establish game preserves by contract on private lands. The Pennsylvania commission set aside a preserve in Center County for the protection of elk, deer, and other game, and this reservation has already been stocked with a herd of 10 elk secured from a private preserve.

Montana created the Sun River Game Preserve in the Lewis and Clark National Forest; Oregon, the Imnaha, Deschutes, Steen's Mountain, Sturgeon Lake, Capitol, and Grass Mountain Preserves; South Dakota, a preserve in Custer County and appropriated $15,000 for fencing and stocking it; Utah, the Strawberry Valley and Fish Lake State game preserves; Washington, a preserve near Commencement Bay on Puget Sound; and Wyoming modified the boundaries of the Teton and Big Horn preserves and established three new refuges known as the Laramie, Popo Agie, and Shoshone preserves. In Canada, the Riding Mountain, Spruce Woods, Turtle Mountain, and Duck Mountain game preserves were created in Manitoba.

BIG GAME.

Several important changes have been made in provisions protecting big game. Colorado and North Dakota prohibited all killing of deer for a term of years and Saskatchewan has provided a close season throughout the year for all big game south of latitude 52°. Laws protecting does at all seasons were enacted in Florida, Nevada, and Wyoming, but South Dakota repealed a statute of this kind enacted in 1911. The deer seasons were shortened from two weeks to two months in Utah, Wyoming, and Quebec. New Hampshire lengthened the season two weeks in Coos County, Vermont ten days, and Massachusetts opened the season in the few closed counties, thus permitting shooting throughout the State. Montana provided that the limit of three deer a season can include only one doe. In 1911 Michigan made an experiment of an open season of 45 days on deer but limited the life of an individual hunting license to 25 days from date of issuance. After a trial of two years the season has been restored to the last three weeks in November to correspond with the deer season in Minnesota and Wisconsin.

Wyoming and Montana, heretofore affording the principal hunting for elk and sheep, have recently limited the hunting area to a few counties in each State, where the seasons have generally been shortened. Wyoming has adopted the innovation of allowing the killing of female elk only under ordinary resident licenses and requiring licensees to obtain a special $15 license to kill a bull or an additional cow. Montana also prohibited the killing of ewes and lambs. Other States in which elk or sheep were protected for a term of years or by a perpetual close season are Nevada, Oregon, Utah, and Washington.

OPEN SEASONS.

The most important changes in seasons are due to the passage of the Federal law protecting migratory birds. Under the regulations as proposed by the Department of Agriculture (see pp. 20–21), spring shooting is entirely eliminated and the open seasons materially shortened in several States.

The general trend of State legislation in the matter of seasons seems to have been toward further restriction of hunting and greater uniformity. This fact is illustrated by the enactment of the general game law in Florida, which repealed all local game laws and made the seasons uniform throughout the State, and the passage of a measure in Wisconsin adopting the same opening date for upland game as is in force in Minnesota and North Dakota. A few important species were removed from the game list or were given protection for shore birds, rail, and geese, and west of the Cascades curtailed the season on ducks 17 days. New Jersey shortened the open season 26 days on upland game and 19 days on woodcock, while Pennsylvania cut down the woodcock season two weeks. In Utah, 45 days were taken off the open season on sage hens and in Wyoming one month on sage grouse and two months on ducks and geese.

At least six States passed laws lengthening open seasons. Illinois added a week for hunting prairie chickens; Michigan, 15 days for ruffed grouse and spruce hens, and 45 days for shore birds and rail; Oregon, 16 days for ducks east of the Cascades; and Vermont, 16 days for ruffed grouse and woodcock and two weeks for plover.

In California several changes in seasons were caused by transfer of certain counties from one game district to another. In this transfer a peculiar condition arose in San Joaquin County. The open season on deer in this county began July 1, as in other counties in District No. 4, but on August 11 the new law went into effect transferring the county to District No. 3, where the open season for deer did not begin until August 15. Consequently the season was closed for three days, August 12, 13, and 14, but opened again on the 15th and continued until October 31. These district changes also account for several differences in the open seasons for doves and quail.

EXPORT AND SALE.

The restrictions on native wild game have a tendency to increase, while those on game imported into the United States or raised in captivity or on private preserves are becoming more liberal.

The sale of imported game was permitted or facilitated in Colorado, Montana, New Jersey, Oregon, and Wyoming, while Arizona repealed the provision permitting the sale of imported game by hotels and restaurants.

The industry of rearing game in private preserves received impetus in the form of legislation permitting the sale of game raised in captivity in Minnesota, New Jersey, and Oregon, but Maine repealed the provision permitting sale of game raised in private preserves.

The sale of all protected game was prohibited in Nevada, Oregon, and Wyoming, while New Jersey enacted provisions similar to those of the New York law prohibiting the sale of all game belonging to a family any species or subspecies of which is native to and protected by the State law.

Other interesting sale provisions are the continued suspension of sale of deer in southeastern Alaska until August 15, 1914, and the prohibition in Pennsylvania of the sale of quail and ruffed grouse wherever taken.

Michigan permitted transportation and sale of rabbits lawfully killed and the sale and export of deerskins or green or mounted buck deer heads under permit; while Vermont permitted deer to be sold during the open season and for a "reasonable time thereafter" and rabbits during the open season.

The legislation of the year shows a decided tendency to place more stringent restrictions on the export of native game. Wyoming prohibited the export of all protected game; Maine reduced the export limit of partridges under a resident license tag from 6 to 5; Ohio reduced the export limit under a nonresident license from 50 to 25 birds and animals, while Maine increased the export limit on ducks under nonresident license from 10 to 15, and permitted a nonresident to export one pair of game birds a month under a 50-cent tag; Michigan restored the provision permitting a nonresident to export one deer under permit and license, and New York required nonresidents to obtain permits to export deer.

BAG LIMITS.

The changes in bag limits tend as usual toward further restrictions. Some novel features in weekly limits were enacted in the Northwest, where in an effort to forestall large week-end bags of birds, Washington provided that the week should end at midnight Wednesday night, and Oregon provided limits for seven consecutive days.

In the case of big game, Washington reduced the limit on sheep and goats from two to one each, and Wyoming now permits only one female elk under each ordinary resident license. In the case of deer, Florida and Oregon reduced the limits from five to three; Montana provided that the limit of three deer shall not include more than one doe; Wyoming reduced the number of deer from two to one, and Maine from two to one in Androscoggin County.

With these restrictions, deer hunting, as shown in the accompanying map, is now permitted in 36 States, 12 of which limit the hunter to one deer a season, and 10 to two. In only about a quarter of the

States is the limit three or more. In Florida, Georgia, Montana, Oregon, and Texas, three; in Louisiana, Mississippi, and South Carolina, five; in Alaska, six; in Alabama and Missouri, one a day; and in Kentucky, Virginia, Arkansas, and North Carolina, no limits except in a few counties in the last two States.

In the case of small game, Vermont reduced the limit on rabbits from six to five a day, and Long Island placed a limit of six a day on varying hares and cottontails.

Among the important reductions in bag limits on birds may be mentioned Missouri, which reduced the daily limit from 25 to 10 and the limit allowed in possession at one time from 50 to 15. Vermont reduced the limit on ruffed grouse, partridge, and woodcock from

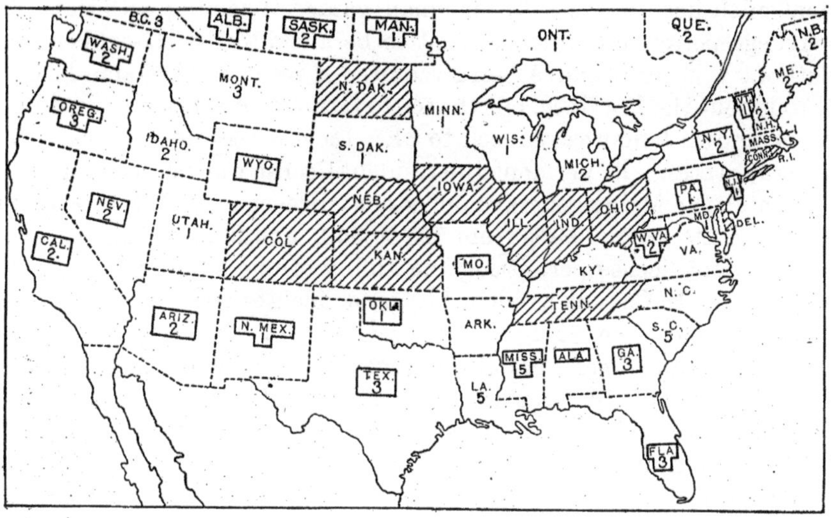

FIG. 1.—States and Provinces permitting deer hunting in 1913.

[In the shaded States there is no deer hunting. Figures indicate the number of deer allowed each hunter a season. In the eastern half of Maine and the southern half of New Hampshire, the limit is one a season. In Alabama, Mississippi, and Missouri, the limit is one a day, and in Louisiana, two. In Arkansas and North Carolina limits are provided in a few counties only. No limits are provided in Kentucky and Virginia. Inclosed names indicate the States which protect does at all seasons.]

5 to 4. In Delaware the limit on rail was reduced from 75 to 50 a day, plover from 15 to 5, and sandpipers from 75 to 50. Washington, while repealing the daily limit on waterfowl, reduced the weekly limit from 50 to 20, and on upland game birds from 30 to 25. Wyoming increased the daily bag limit on geese only from 5 to 12. In Canada, Saskatchewan established limits of 50 a day and 250 a season on waterfowl. In new bag limits, Long Island provided a limit of 10 quail a day—50 a season; and 4 ruffed grouse a day—20 a season; while Utah established limits of 6 a day, and 25 a year on grouse.

LICENSES.

License measures received consideration in 16 States and 4 Canadian Provinces, and resident licenses were adopted for the first time in Delaware, Florida, Michigan (birds), Ohio, and Pennsylvania. The fee in each instance is $1 with additions of 10 to 25 cents as a clerk fee in Delaware, Ohio, and Pennsylvania. Alberta also required a $1.25 bird license for residents of cities in the southern part of the Province. Other new license requirements were as follows: Maine provided a special nonresident license (fee $5) for hunting birds in certain counties prior to October 1; Michigan a nonresident and resident alien license (fee $10) for small game; Wyoming withdrew the privilege permitting a nonresident to be afield with a .22-caliber rifle without a license; and Alberta required a resident big game license throughout the Province, but the fee to farmers and their sons residing on their own land was reduced to $1. License fees were increased in several States. In Vermont the resident license was raised from 50 to 75 cents; the Maine general nonresident license from $15 to $25; in Montana the general alien from $25 to $30; and in Wyoming the special resident license permitting the killing of one additional elk from $5 to $15. In Canada resident big game licenses were increased from $2 to $3 and from $2 to $5, respectively, in New Brunswick and Saskatchewan. Fees were also reduced in three Western States: in Utah the cost of the alien license was reduced from $100 to $15; in Wyoming, the alien bird license, from $20 to $5, and the resident bird license from $1.50 to $1; and in Washington the $5 nonresident county licenses and the $50 nonresident alien licenses were abolished.

Montana and Oregon required $25 alien gun licenses in addition to the prescribed hunting licenses, but on the whole the license legislation affecting aliens has been more favorable than usual.

Among the miscellaneous provisions the following may be mentioned: Massachusetts, Wisconsin, and Wyoming strengthened their license laws; New Hampshire authorized town clerks to issue resident licenses, but in order to prevent fraudulent issue of such licenses to nonresidents prohibited issue to any applicant not personally known to the clerk as a resident of the State.

WARDEN SERVICE.

The warden service of at least 17 States was affected either directly or indirectly by the legislation of the year and in most instances the tendency was to increase its effectiveness. Florida created the office of fish and game commissioner, Maine delegated the protection of game on the islands in the sea and 1 mile inland on the coast to the department of sea and shore fisheries, Wyoming authorized the appointment of employees of the department of agriculture as deputy game wardens without bond or salary, and Wisconsin authorized the State warden to assign deputies for educational work in regard to fish and game. The service has been reorganized in several States. In Montana, South Dakota, and Illinois commissions, instead of single officers, were formed in charge of the work of game preservation; in Ohio an agricultural commission was established to replace several State departments and the game warden department placed under its charge; in Connecticut the personnel of the fish and game commission was increased to include a member from each of the eight counties of the State, while New Hampshire was the only State which abolished its fish and game commission and placed the work in charge of a single officer. Delaware established the resident and nonresident license system, thus providing funds for the operation and maintenance of the game commission created in 1911. Arkansas, Mississippi, Nevada, and Virginia are now the only States which have no State officials in charge of the work of game protection.

Increase in salaries of game officials were granted in several States. In Arizona the compensation of the warden was increased from \$1,200 to \$1,800, with an allowance of \$1,000 for traveling expenses; in Iowa from \$1,600 to \$2,200; in Utah from \$1,800 to \$2,400; in Wisconsin from \$2,000 to \$2,500; and in Illinois the president of the commission was given \$4,000. Deputies were also provided for in some cases. Arizona created the position of office deputy at a salary of \$1,200, provided that warden salaries and expenses should be paid from the general fund of the State, and authorized the appointment of such per diem deputies as might be necessary. Vermont appropriated \$2,500 for clerical assistance for the biennial period, and Utah increased the salary of the chief deputy from \$1,200 to \$1,400, Washington from \$1,500 to \$1,800, and Wyoming authorized the appointment of a clerk in the warden department at \$1,200 a year and increased the compensation of county wardens from \$3 to \$5 per day. Iowa authorized the appointment of three assistant game wardens at \$1,200 per annum each; North Dakota increased the warden force by authorizing the appointment of one regular deputy for each judicial district instead of four for each commission district, while South Dakota provided for the appointment of three salaried wardens and five assistant per diem game wardens in lieu of the former county wardens. In Oklahoma the salaried warden system of 12 deputies was abolished, thus limiting the service to assistant wardens, who serve on a fee basis and without other compensation.

RETROGRADE LEGISLATION.

Among the retrograde legislation of the year may be mentioned the Colorado provision extending spring shooting, the repeal of the Massachusetts provision allowing dogs chasing deer to be killed, the Maine prohibition of sale of game raised in private preserves, the suspension of salaried warden service in Oklahoma, and the repeal of the South Dakota doe law. Game protection funds were diverted to other purposes in New Hampshire by a provision that the surplus shall be devoted to screening ponds and forestry work, and in Florida by the requirement that funds in excess of $5,000 on March 1 of each year shall be turned over to the State school fund.

More than the usual number of game laws have been the subject of vetoes, notably in Wisconsin, where a bill prohibiting aliens from hunting failed to receive the approval of the governor, and in California, where two bills removing the band-tailed pigeon and certain shore birds from the game list were vetoed. The only law apparently in which the referendum was invoked was the California statute prohibiting the sale of game but allowing sale of ducks in November.

PRESENT CONDITION OF GAME LEGISLATION.

As an illustration of the progress of game legislation and the general adoption of certain provisions in the various States, a comparison may be made between conditions in 1900 (the date of the passage of the Lacey act, the first Federal law) and those of to-day. Every one of the 48 States now prescribes seasons for hunting, prohibits export of game, and requires nonresidents to secure a license. Only one State is without some restriction on sale of game, 4 are without State game wardens or commissioners, 5 have no general bag-limit laws, 9 do not issue resident hunting licenses, and 9 have not yet adopted the so-called "model law" for the protection of nongame birds. The progress in each of these features is shown by the following table:

Table showing condition of game legislation in 1900 and 1913.

Provisions.	Number of States. 1900	Number of States. 1913	States lacking legislation.
Seasons	48	48	
Export	41	48	
Nonresident license	15	48	
Sale	28	47	(1) North Carolina.
State warden	31	44	(4) Arkansas, Mississippi, Nevada, Virginia.
Limits	20	43	(5) Arkansas, Kentucky, North Carolina, Rhode Island, Virginia.
Resident license	5	39	(9) Arkansas, Maine, Maryland, Mississippi, North Carolina, South Carolina, Tennessee, Virginia, West Virginia.
Nongame birds (model law)	7	39	(9) Arizona, Idaho, Kansas, Maryland, Montana, Nevada, Nebraska, New Mexico, Utah.

NEW LAWS PASSED IN 1913.

FEDERAL LAWS.

Two acts: Agricultural appropriation act containing provisions for Federal protection of migratory birds and for the establishment and maintenance of elk refuge in Wyoming (37 Stat., 847); resolution authorizing the President to propose to Governments of other countries the negotiation of a convention for the protection and preservation of birds (S. Res. 25.)

FEDERAL REGULATIONS.

Proposed regulations of the Department of Agriculture under the law for the protection of migratory birds (Biol. Circ. 92); regulations of August 1 under the Alaska game law suspending the sale of deer in Alaska until August 15, 1914, and shortening the season on mountain goats.

STATE LAWS.

Arkansas.—Four acts: Affecting Boone, Calhoun, Grant, Hot Spring, Lonoke, and Monroe counties (Acts 251, 267, 276, 280).

Arizona.—One act: Prohibiting the importation of game for sale; repealing the provision authorizing the State warden to appoint per diem State deputies; increasing the salary of the State warden from $1,200 to $1,800, allowing $1,000 per year for traveling expenses, and authorizing the appointment of an office deputy at $1,200 per year, all to be paid from the general fund; making sheriffs, constables, and live-stock sanitary inspectors ex officio game wardens; authorizing the State warden to appoint such county deputy game wardens as may be necesssary at $3 per diem and expenses while under directions from the State warden.

California.—Several laws; not received at date of going to press.

Colorado.—Two acts: Protecting deer until 1918 and imported pheasants until 1924; lengthening the open season on waterfowl, cranes, and shore birds (except curlew and yellowlegs) 81 days, and on curlews and yellowlegs 112 days; shortening the season on doves two weeks and making it uniform throughout the State (ch. —); memorializing Congress to enact Senate bill 6497 for the protection of migratory game and insectivorous birds (H. J. M. No. 3).

Connecticut.—Six acts: Providing that any licensed hunter who shall injure fences or let down bars without replacing them shall forfeit his hunting license and the privilege of securing another license for a period of two years (ch. 37); shortening the season on rabbits three weeks, making it open on the same date as the season for upland game (ch. 74); prohibiting use of snares for all game (ch. 79); requiring applicants for hunting license to be 16 years old (ch. 103); permitting killing of the starling, and red-winged and crow blackbirds when destroying corn (ch. 133); providing for the appointment of a nonpartisan commission of eight members, one from each county, and the appointment of a superintendent of fisheries and game (ch. 228).

Delaware.—Seven acts: Providing resident and nonresident hunting licenses with fees of $1.10 and $10.50, respectively (ch. 152); closing the season indefinitely on Hungarian partridges, pheasants (ch. 156), and swans in the State and on doves in Newcastle County and reducing the daily limit on rail from 75 to 50 (ch. 158); shortening the seasons on squirrels two months, on ducks one month, and on geese and brant two weeks, and making the season on waterfowl uniform in the State (ch. 159); authorizing the appointment of a chief game and fish warden, salary $600 per annum (ch. 153); providing that all fines shall be paid into the game protection fund (ch. 154); increasing the weekly export limit on birds from 1 dozen to 20 and on animals from 6 to 10 of each species and repealing the shipping exemption in favor of residents on plover, snipe, and ducks; requiring officers of any court to remit fines collected to the commission, and abolishing the informer's fee and the provision that part of the fines shall go to the Audubon Society (ch. 155).

Florida.—Three acts: A general game law, making seasons on all game uniform throughout the State, prohibiting the killing of does and hen turkeys at any time and ruffed grouse and imported pheasants until December 1, 1915; prohibiting export and sale of all protected game, reducing the bag limit on deer from five to three a year, providing daily and yearly limits on birds, and repealing all local laws (ch. 6534); creating the office of game and fish commissioner at a salary of $2,500 and establishing $1 county and $3 State licenses for residents and a $15 county license for nonresidents and aliens, creating a game and fish protection fund and providing that any surplus above $5,000 in said fund shall be paid March 1 each year into the State school fund (ch. 6535). Extending absolute protection to robins (ch. 6533). A number of local game laws were passed but were all repealed by the provision in ch. 6534.

Georgia.—No legislation.

Idaho.—No legislation.

Illinois.—One act: Replacing the office of State game commissioner by a State game and fish conservation commission of three members, the president to receive a salary of $4,000, the other two members $3,000 each; authorizing the appointment of six wardens at $1,500 and 60 deputy wardens at $1,200 a year each, and additional deputies for temporary services at $100 per month; shortening the open season on squirrels one month and on doves six weeks; lengthening the season on prairie chickens one week; extending the close term until 1918 on partridge, blue, mountain, and valley quail, Hungarian partridge, capercailzie, heath hen, black grouse, and woodcock, and until 1923 on wild turkey, sand grouse, and imported pheasants and partridges; and providing that all license receipts shall be paid into the State treasury (S. B. 617).

Indiana.—Four acts: Prohibiting the use of ferrets in hunting rabbits (ch. 12); repealing the provision requiring one-third of the license receipts to be expended for restocking purposes and providing that all license receipts shall be paid into a fish and game fund (ch. 120); shortening the open season on quail and ruffed grouse 10 days, extending protection to rabbits from January 10 to April 1, and prohibiting the hunting of any other game from December 20 to April 1; reducing the commissioner's fee taxed against the defendant under the game laws from $20 to $5 (ch. 147); removing protection from blackbirds and increasing the maximum penalty for violation of the nongame bird law from $25 to $50 (ch. 197).

Iowa.—Two acts: Increasing the salary of the game warden from $1,600 to $2,200 and authorizing the appointment of three assistant game wardens at $1,200 a year each (ch. 203); providing that no deer shall be distrained until it shall be necessary in the opinion of the game warden or his deputies (ch. 206).

Kansas.—Two acts: Protecting quail and prairie chicken for five years, adding doves to the game list without a season, but providing a limit of 20 a day; increasing the limit on plover and ducks from 12 each to 20 each a day (ch. —); authorizing the issue of permits to export game birds for scientific or propagating purposes (ch. —).

Maine.—One act: General revision and codification of game and fish laws; shortening the season on bull moose two weeks; protecting deer on Mount Desert Island, shifting the season in Androscoggin County, and making it more uniform in the State; repealing the provision authorizing the commission to reimburse farmers and tenants for damage done by deer; extending complete protection to Hungarian partridges; pheasants, black game, and capercailzie, (cock of the woods); making the law on ducks uniform throughout the State; reducing the daily bag on plover from 15 to 5. on snipe and ducks from 15 to 10, and on sandpipers from 70 to 50; removing protection from the mudhen (bittern), kingfisher, loon, and blue heron; increasing the fee for a nonresident general license from $15 to $25, and providing special $5 licenses for hunting birds prior to October 1 and November 1 in certain parts of the State; increasing the export limit of ducks under a nonresident license from 10 to 15; permitting nonresident licensee to export one pair of game birds a month, unaccompanied, under a 50-cent tag; making the appointment of inland deputies expire with the calendar year in which made; prohibiting the sale of game raised in private preserves; and extending the jurisdiction of the department of sea and shore fisheries to all islands along the coast of the State and to a distance of 1 mile inland, including all bays and inlets so far as the tide ebbs and flows except on the Kennebec River above the city of Bath (ch. 206).

Massachusetts.—Nine acts: Strengthening the license law (ch. 249); shifting the season on gray squirrels to make it uniform with that on upland game birds (ch. 270); authorizing city and town councils to protect insectivorous birds and to appoint bird wardens (ch. 296); extending the license exemption in favor of certain nonresident taxpayers to their minor children over 18 years of age (ch. 479); opening the season throughout the State on deer (ch. 529); prohibiting the use of rifle, revolver, or pistol for hunting any game (ch. 542); providing a penalty of $20 for knowingly permitting a dog to chase deer (ch. 552); prohibiting the poisoning and snaring of wild animals (ch. 626), and extending protection to moose throughout the year (ch. 744).

Michigan.—Eight acts: Protecting the snowy heron and prohibiting sale of its plumage (No. 22); removing protection from black bears (No. 83); prescribing $1 resident and $10 nonresident licenses for small game (No. 108); permitting the transportation and sale of rabbits lawfully killed, and sale and export of deer skins or green or mounted buck deer heads under permit; reducing the daily bag on plover from 10 to 6; shortening the season on deer 23 days, and on woodcock 16 days; extending the close term on squirrels to 1915, and that on quail, English and Mongolian pheasants, black game, capercailzie, hazel grouse, and wild turkeys to 1917; lengthening the season on rabbits 45 days, on ruffed grouse and spruce hens 15 days; on ducks, snipe, plover, shorebirds, and sora rail 45 days; and on coots and other rail one month, and permitting nonresident licensees to export one deer under permit (No. 167); establishing a game preserve on the new maneuvering grounds of the State militia in Crawford County (No. 172); increasing the salary of the chief deputy from $1,500 to $1,800, providing for the appointment of deputies at salaries from $2.50 to $4 a day, with promotions on a merit basis after examination (No. 313); amending form of deer licenses and affidavits and requiring licenses to be issued in stated distinctive colors (No. 328); and authorizing the establishment of game preserves on private holdings and State forests (No. 360).

Minnesota.—Eight acts: Repealing the law prohibiting the use of ferrets for rabbits in certain counties (ch. 5); prohibiting the use of silencers (ch. 64); protecting game on lands designated by commission as game propagating and breeding grounds (ch. 95); permitting game birds to be raised in captivity under permit and sold when properly tagged (ch. 131); protecting squirrels on all public grounds and within one-quarter mile thereof (ch. 133); prohibiting shooting of waterfowl from one hour after sunset to one hour before sunrise (ch. 212); permitting big game raised in private preserves to be killed and sold at any time under permit (ch. 485); memorializing Congress to afford protection to migratory game bids (J. Res. No. 13).

Missouri.—Four acts: Shortening the season on quail one month (p. 346); on squirrels three weeks (p. 347); reducing the daily limit on birds from 25 to 10 and the number allowed in possession at one time from 50 to 15 (p. 348); and prohibiting the use of dogs for hunting deer (p. 346).

Montana.—Eight acts: Making all licenses expire on April 30 of each year (ch. 31); protecting elk until 1918 except in certain counties, and prohibiting the killing of fawns, ewes, and lambs (ch. 33); establishing the Sun River Game Preserves in Lewis and Clark National Forest (ch. 34); requiring certain aliens to obtain a $25 gun license (ch. 38); classifying hunting and fishing licenses; increasing the fee of an alien general license from $25 to $30; creating the Montana game and fish commission to consist of the State warden, and four unsalaried members appointed by the governor, term four years; permitting common carriers to transport fish, game, and birds for restocking, and agents of State or Federal Government prosecuting such work in the State free of charge or at reduced rates, and providing that not more than one doe shall be included in the limit of deer (ch. 79); authorizing the appointment of six additional special deputy game and fish wardens, at a salary of $1,500 a year each with expenses not to exceed $900 a year (ch. 96); permitting merchants, hotel, or restaurant keepers to sell under transportation receipt game that has been killed outside the State (ch. 100); defining the term "sale" of game and fish (ch. 126).

Nebraska.—No legislation.

Nevada.—Four acts: Authorizing board of county commissioners, upon receipt of petition of 25 residents, to open the season on sandhill crane, shore birds, and waterfowl September 1 (ch. 78); prohibiting sale of all protected game except sandhill crane and swan (ch. 241); protecting mountain sheep and goats until 1920 (ch. 252); shortening the season on grouse two weeks, shifting the season on deer to open a month later and prohibiting the killing of does, and authorizing county commissioners upon petition to change and shift open seasons (ch. 265).

New Hampshire.—Four acts: Lengthening the open season on deer two weeks in Coos County (ch. 63); making it unlawful to allow self-hunting dogs to run at large between April 1 and October 1 in woods or fields inhabited by game (ch. 143); replacing the board of fish and game commissioners by a single commissioner in charge of game and fish preservation at a salary of $1,800 per annum and reducing the term of office from five to three years; authorizing the biennial appointment of one deputy in each county at a compensation of $3 and expenses for each day of actual service; reducing the fee for issuing resident hunting licenses from 25 to 10 cents; providing that any surplus from the proceeds of fines and hunting licenses shall be devoted to screening ponds and to forestry work (ch. 165); extending the protection on gray squirrels until 1919, but permitting shooting during the month of October outside thickly settled parts of cities and towns (ch. 174).

New Jersey.—Seven acts: Prohibiting the hunting of wild fowl from any sand bar not covered with water (ch. 73); shortening the season on upland game 26 days (ch. 120); permitting the sale under tags of game raised in preserves (ch. 135); permitting certain pheasants, ducks, and deer to be raised in inclosed preserves under license (ch. 147); authorizing game commissioners and protectors to file complaints on "information and belief" (ch. 148); prohibiting use of hounds in hunting except during the open season for quail (ch. 157).

New Mexico.—No legislation.

New York.—One act: Lengthening the season on varying hares and rabbits one month; shifting the season on squirrels; closing the season on quail until 1918; shortening the season one month on varying hares and cottontail rabbits on Long Island; permitting nonresident licenses to export one deer under permit; permitting game raised in captivity to be killed and sold at any time under license; providing the following bag limits for Long Island, 10 quail, 4 ruffed grouse, and 6 varying hares or cottontail rabbits a day, 50 quail, and 20 ruffed grouse a season; and making numerous technical amendments to the conservation law (ch. 508).

North Carolina.—Numerous local laws; not received at date of going to press.

North Dakota.—One act: Authorizing the appointment of one regular deputy warden for each judicial district (instead of four for each commission district); closing the season on deer until 1916, prohibiting spring shooting of geese and cranes, and adding all the year protection to partridge.

Ohio.—Three acts: Removing quail, ruffed grouse, and doves from the game list by closing the season until 1915; extending the protection on imported pheasants to 1915; closing the open season on shorebirds, rails, coots, and waterfowl December 1 (No. 79); creating the agricultural commission and delegating to it the work of game preservation (No. 147); providing a resident license, fee $1.25, and requiring licensee to wear a badge conspicuously exposed bearing the number of his hunting license; creating a game-protection fund into which all license receipts shall be paid; authorizing the expenditure of 50 per cent of the game fund for the purposes of restocking, and the establishment of game preserves on private holdings; and reducing the export limit under a nonresident license from 50 to 25 birds or animals (No. 249).

Oklahoma.—Two acts: Opening the season on male deer in Delaware County (ch. —); abolishing the salaried-warden system and the present force of 12 wardens.

Oregon.—Five acts: General revision of the game and fish laws—Dividing the State into two game districts, east and west of the Cascades; extending absolute protection to elk, caribou, and goats; affording protection throughout the year to imported pheasants and partridges, bobwhite, prairie chicken, wild turkey, certain shore birds, and swan; shortening the season on doves and wild pigeons 46 days, on shore birds, rail, coot, and geese 6 weeks, and on ducks west of Cascades 17 days, but east of Cascades lengthening the season 16 days; protecting squirrels east of Cascades all the year; reducing the limit on deer from 5 to 3; making numerous changes in local bag limits; providing limits for seven consecutive days instead of individual weekly limits; prohibiting the sale of all game, except imported game, between September 1 and November 1, and game birds or animals raised in captivity under permit and tag; establishing civil liability for game illegally killed; providing a $25 alien gun license; permitting game to be raised in captivity under permit; removing protection from cormorants, American mergansers, and ravens, and prohibiting use of a gun larger than 10 gauge (ch. 232); creating the Imnaha, Deschutes, Steen's Mountain, Sturgeon Lake, Capitol, and Grass Mountain game preserves (ch. 189); permitting such exceptions in contracts for the establishment of game preserves on private lands as will protect the property or crops of the owner (ch. 251); resolution requesting Federal protection of migratory game birds (S. J. M. No. 2); resolution requesting enactment of a law establishing Federal refuges for the protection of big game (S. J. M. No. 6).

Pennsylvania.—Seven acts: Removing doves, killdeer plover, and blackbirds from the game list (No. 11); protecting elk until 1921, but permitting them to be raised in captivity under the same regulations as apply to deer (No. 26); prescribing a resident license, fee $1.15, and requiring each licensee to wear the number of his license on back of his sleeve (No. 63); shifting the season on squirrels, ruffed grouse, and imported pheasants two weeks earlier; shortening the season on woodcock two weeks, lengthening the season on rabbits and Hungarian partridges two weeks (No. 70); amending the nongame bird law by extending protection to the shrike, eagle, osprey, crane, heron, bittern, and raven, and prohibiting the sale of plumage of native birds or any foreign birds of the same family, in effect July 1, 1914 (No. 72); protecting wild turkeys until 1915 (No. 123); prohibiting the sale of quail and ruffed grouse wherever taken (No. 134).

Rhode Island.—One act: Shifting the season on quail, ruffed grouse, and woodcock two weeks, to open November 1 instead of October 15, and protecting imported pheasants and Hungarian partridges until 1920 (ch. 966).

South Carolina.—No legislation.

South Dakota.—Five acts: Creating a State game and fish commission to consist of the governor, attorney general, and the State game warden, and providing for the employment of one clerk, three assistant salaried wardens, and five assistant per diem game wardens (supplanting the county game-warden system), and providing rewards for informers (ch. 223); establishing a State game preserve in Custer County and appropriating $15,000 for fencing and stocking it (ch. 224); extending absolute protection to quail (ch. 225); creating a game fund (ch. 226); repealing the protection afforded does in 1911 and permitting them to be killed during the regular open season (ch. 227).

Tennessee.—Four local laws: Protecting game in Haywood, Johnson, Lauderdale, Washington, and Unicoi Counties (chs. 117, 269, 271, 309).

Texas.—**No legislation.**

Utah.—Two acts: General revision of the game laws: Increasing salary of the commissioner from $1,800 to $2,400 and that of the chief deputy from $1,200 to $1,400 per annum; shortening the season two weeks on deer, 45 days on sage hens, on quail in certain counties, and providing an open season of 10 days on grouse and a limit of 6 a day and 25 a year; providing a close season throughout the year for elk, antelope, sheep, doves, shore birds (except snipe), and swans; increasing the daily limit on geese from 5 to 12; affording protection throughout the year to pelicans, bitterns, hawks, blackbirds, and kingfishers; reducing the fee for an alien license from $100 to $15; creating the Strawberry Valley and Fish Lake game preserves; authorizing the commissioner with concurrence of the State board of examiners, to set aside and maintain public hunting grounds in Salt Lake, Davis, and Box Elder Counties (ch. 46); and providing for the observance of bird day in the schools on the last Friday in April of each year (ch. 60).

Vermont.—Five acts: General revision and codification of the game laws; lengthening the season on deer 10 days, on ruffed grouse and woodcock 16 days, and on plover and English snipe two weeks; providing a close season on other shore birds for the first time, December 1 to September 1, and providing no open season for pheasants, European partridges, upland plover, and wood duck; permitting the sale of deer and rabbits during the open season and of deer for a "reasonable time thereafter;" increasing the resident license fee from 50 to 75 cents; reducing the daily bag on rabbits from 6 to 5 and limiting possession of rabbits and squirrels to one day's bag; reducing the daily limit on quail, ruffed grouse, partridge, and woodcock from 5 to 4 each, and that on plover and English snipe from 5 each a day to 10 of all shore birds combined; authorizing the commissioner to seize and confiscate birds or quadrupeds held in violation of law, and wardens to search without warrant; providing for the establishment of private preserves, game refuges, and regulation of propagation farms (No. 201); relating to rabbits (No. 205); trapping and other prohibited methods of taking game (No. 206); protecting elk for 10 years (No. 208); appropriating $2,500 for clerical assistance of the commissioner for the biennial period (J. Res. No. 496).

Washington.—Three acts: Creating a county game commission of three resident members for each county and providing for the appointment of a chief game warden west of the Cascades and a chief deputy warden east of the Cascades; county commission authorized to appoint wardens and assistants and to set aside by proper publication county game preserves; shifting the season on big game to open October 1 instead of September 1; protecting moose until 1925, and allowing no open season for caribou and swan, with numerous changes in local seasons, tending slightly toward uniformity; reducing the seasonal limit on sheep and goat from 2 to 1 each, and on upland game birds from 30 a week to 25; omitting the daily limit on waterfowl, reducing the weekly limit from 50 to 20, and defining a week to begin at midnight on Wednesday night; repealing the nonresident $5 county license and the $50 alien license (ch. 120); creating a game refuge in Pierce County, near Commencement Bay, on Puget Sound (ch. 122).

West Virginia.—One act: Protecting elk until 1928 (ch. 27).

Wisconsin.—Nineteen acts: Reimbursing the warden and deputies for certain expenditures incurred in the line of duty (chs. 19, 24, 29, 498, and 499); extending absolute protection to deer in Door, and in Wood County until 1916 (ch. 46); permitting use of ferrets for taking rabbits on hunter's own land in Door County (ch. 71); authorizing the prosecution of educational work in behalf of fish and game by the game warden and his deputies (ch. 73); more clearly defining the term "nighttime," during which wild fowl are protected as the period from one hour after sunset to one hour before sunrise central time (ch. 97); granting a clerk fee of 10 cents for issuing resident licenses (ch. 172); permitting shipment or export to a taxidermist of green deer heads when severed from the carcass, under permit from warden (ch. 258); directing superintendent of public property to provide suitable quarters for the warden department (ch. 369); regarding local protection of rabbits and squirrels (chs. 403 and 104); strengthening the license law (ch. 424); authorizing the printing of 3,000 copies of the report of the State fish and game warden (ch. 429); making the seasons for game birds open on the same dates as those in Minnesota and North Dakota (ch. 737); protecting elk indefinitely (ch. 748); and memorializing Congress to set aside unoccupied and unclaimed islands in the Great Lakes for bird reserves (J. Res. 63–A).

Wyoming.—One act: General revision; enlarging powers of game warden and deputies, permitting employees of the U. S. Department of Agriculture to be appointed deputy game wardens without bond or pay; extending term protection to quail and Mongolian pheasants until 1915; shortening the season on deer 2 months, on grouse 4 days, and on sage grouse 1 month; extending term protection to moose, elk, and sheep until 1918, except in three counties in the northwest part of the State, where the season on elk and male sheep was shortened 15 days; repealing the provision permitting nonresidents to be afield with a .22-caliber rifle without a license; reducing the fee for the alien bird license from $20 to $5; prohibiting the sale or possession of game taken in a State, nation, or foreign country when such acts are prohibited in this State; requiring soldiers and sailors stationed at Government posts in the State when hunting to be accompanied by a qualified guide; reducing the clerk fees for issuing licenses; regulating sale and export; modifying the boundary lines of the Teton and Big Horn game preserves and creating the Popo Agie, Shoshone, and Laramie game preserves; increasing the pay of county deputy game wardens from $3 to $5 a day; increasing the fee for a resident special license for one additional elk from $5 to $15; and reducing the fee for a resident bird license from $1.50 to $1; reducing the limit on deer from two to one male, and under a resident ordinary license from two elk to one female elk; authorizing the appointment of a clerk in the office of the State warden at a salary of $1,200; reducing the daily limit of grouse from 12 to 6; and prohibiting the use of a silencer (ch. 121).

CANADIAN LAWS.

Alberta.—One act: Protecting elk until 1915; permitting the sale of all game birds except those of the grouse family September 20 to March 1; making the resident big game license apply throughout the Province, but requiring a fee of only $1 of farmers and their sons residing on their own land; reducing the fee for a market hunter's license from $10 to $5; prescribing a $1.25 bird license for residents of city or town south of township 59; permitting treaty Indians to hunt without license.

Manitoba.—One act: Permitting all game except pheasants to be taken at any time north of latitude 54° by persons in actual need of food; prohibiting hunting of waterfowl in yachts or launches propelled by steam, gasoline, or electric motive power; also protecting waterfowl on sand bars or shallow islands in open waters of Whitewater Lake; prohibiting export of big game except by nonresident licensee, lawfully killing same, under permit, fees, deer $2, and moose, elk, and caribou, $5; creating Riding Mountain, Spruce Woods, Turtle Mountain, and Duck Mountain game preserves, and prohibiting all hunting on said preserves except that ducks and geese may be taken during the month of October on Turtle Mountain preserve; and requiring persons hunting big game to wear a white coat or sweater and cap (ch. 21).

New Brunswick.—One act: Shortening the season two weeks on snipe; repealing the provision permitting residents of Grand Manan Parish, Charlotte County, to kill black ducks until May 1; prohibiting the sale of partridges until 1915; and increasing the fee for a resident big game license from $2 to $3.

Newfoundland.—One act: Lengthening the season two weeks on partridge, ptarmigan, willow grouse, plover, curlew, snipe, and other migratory birds.

Ontario.—One act: Repealing the authority of lieutenant governor in council to require nonresident licensees to employ guides while hunting big game and for making regulations for Rondeau Park, and permitting game animals bred in captivity to be possessed and sold at any time under permit.

Quebec.—One act: Shortening the season on moose and deer two months in Labelle and Temiscaming Counties; lengthening the season on hares six weeks; permitting the killing of any game animal injuring or threatening damage to property (but in the case of big game actual damage must have been caused); prohibiting the sale of all game during the first three days of the open season and of birch or swamp partridge until 1917.

Saskatchewan.—One act: Providing no open season for big game south of latitude 52° and shifting the season to open two weeks earlier; shortening the season two weeks on shore birds, rail, and waterfowl and six weeks on cranes; lengthening the season one month on grouse; establishing a bag limit of 50 a day and 250 a season on waterfowl; and prohibiting the killing of waterfowl from yacht or launch propelled by steam, gasoline, or electric motive power; increasing the export fee on big game from $1 to $5 a head; permitting the sale of all game except Gallinæ under a $5 dealer's license; increasing the fee for a resident big-game license from $2 to $5 and requiring holder of said license to wear a complete outer suit and cap of white and fixing a penalty of $500 to $1,000, or six months imprisonment for accidentally shooting a person and shall be ineligible to receive a license for 10 years; authorizing complimentary licenses to be granted to certain Canadian officials; and providing that the game laws shall apply to all Indians whether resident upon a reserve or elsewhere.

SEASONS.

The most important game legislation during the year was undoubtedly the act of Congress protecting migratory birds. In accordance with this act regulations were published by the Department of Agriculture (Cir. No. 92, Bureau of Biological Survey) on June 23, 1913, and if finally adopted will become effective on or after October 1, 1913, when approved by the President. As these regulations modify existing seasons of certain species to a considerable extent, they are published in full although subject to change before final approval.

PROPOSED REGULATIONS FOR THE PROTECTION OF MIGRATORY BIRDS.

Pursuant to the provisions of the act of March 4, 1913, authorizing and directing the Department of Agriculture to adopt suitable regulations prescribing and fixing closed seasons for migratory birds (37 Stat., 847), having due regard to zones of temperature, breeding habits, and times and lines of migratory flight, the Department of Agriculture has adopted the following regulations:

Regulation 1. Definitions.

For the purposes of these regulations the following shall be considered migratory game birds:

(*a*) Anatidæ or waterfowl, including brant, wild ducks, geese, and swans.

(*b*) Gruidæ or cranes, including little brown, sandhill, and whooping cranes.

(*c*) Rallidæ or rails, including coots, gallinules, and sora and other rails.

(*d*) Limicolæ or shore birds, including avocets, curlew, dowitchers, godwits, knots, oyster catchers, phalaropes, plover, sandpipers, snipe, stilts, surf birds, turnstones, willet, woodcock, and yellow legs.

(*e*) Columbidæ or pigeons, including doves and wild pigeons.

For the purposes of these regulations the following shall be considered migratory insectivorous birds:

(*f*) Bobolinks, catbirds, chickadees, cuckoos, flycatchers, grosbeaks, humming birds, kinglets, martins, meadow larks, night hawks or bull bats, nuthatches, orioles, robins, shrikes, swallows, swifts, tanagers, titmice, thrushes, vireos, warblers, waxwings, whippoorwills, woodpeckers, and wrens, and all other perching birds which feed entirely or chiefly on insects.

Regulation 2. Closed seasons at night.

A daily closed season on all migratory game and insectivorous birds shall extend from sunset to sunrise.

Regulation 3. Closed season on insectivorous birds.

A closed season on migratory insectivorous birds shall continue to December 31, 1913, and each year thereafter shall begin January 1 and continue to December 31, both dates inclusive, provided that nothing in this regulation shall be construed to prevent the issue of permits for collecting such birds for scientific purposes in accordance with the laws and regulations in force in the respective States and Territories and the District of Columbia; and provided further that the closed season on reedbirds or ricebirds in Delaware, Maryland, the District of Columbia, Virginia, and South Carolina shall begin November 1 and end August 31 next following, both dates inclusive.

Regulation 4. Five-year Closed Seasons on Certain Game Birds.

A closed season shall continue until September 1, 1918, on the following migratory game birds: Band-tailed pigeons, little brown, sandhill, and whooping cranes, swans, curlew, and all shorebirds except the black-breasted and golden plover, Wilson or jacksnipe, woodcock, and the greater and lesser yellow legs.

A closed season shall also continue until September 1, 1918, on wood ducks in Maine, New Hampshire, Vermont, Massachusetts, Rhode Island, Connecticut, New York, New Jersey, Pennsylvania, Ohio, Indiana, Michigan, West Virginia, and Wisconsin; on rails in California and Vermont; and on woodcock in Illinois and Missouri.

Regulation 5. Closed Season on Certain Navigable Rivers.

A closed season shall continue between January 1 and October 31, both dates inclusive, of each year, on all migratory birds passing over or at rest on any of the waters of the main streams of the following navigable rivers, to wit: The Mississippi River between New Orleans, La., and Minneapolis, Minn.; the Ohio River between its mouth and Pittsburgh, Pa.; and the Missouri River between its mouth and Bismarck, N. Dak.; and on the killing or capture of any of such birds on or over the shores of any of said rivers, or at any point within the limits aforesaid, from any boat, raft, or other device, floating or otherwise, in or on any such waters.

Regulation 6. Zones.

The following zones for the protection of migratory game and insectivorous birds are hereby established:

Zone No. 1, the breeding zone, comprising States lying wholly or in part north of latitude 40° and the Ohio River, and including Maine, New Hampshire, Vermont, Massachusetts, Rhode Island, Connecticut, New York, New Jersey, Pennsylvania, Ohio, Indiana, Illinois, Michigan, Wisconsin, Minnesota, Iowa, North Dakota, South Dakota, Nebraska, Colorado, Wyoming, Montana, Idaho, Oregon, and Washington—25 States.

Zone No. 2, the wintering zone, comprising States lying wholly or in part south of latitude 40° and the Ohio River and including Delaware, Maryland, the District of Columbia, West Virginia, Virginia, North Carolina, South Carolina, Georgia, Florida, Alabama, Mississippi, Tennessee, Kentucky, Missouri, Arkansas, Louisiana, Texas, Oklahoma, Kansas, New Mexico, Arizona, California, Nevada, and Utah—23 States and the District of Columbia.

Regulation 7. Construction.

For the purposes of regulations 8 and 9, each period of time therein prescribed as a closed season shall be construed to include the first day and to exclude the last day thereof.

Regulation 8. Closed Seasons in Zone No. 1.

Closed seasons in zone No. 1 shall be as follows:

Waterfowl.—The closed season on waterfowl shall be between December 16 and September 1 next following, except as follows:

Exceptions: In Massachusetts the closed season shall be between January 1 and September 15.

In Minnesota and North Dakota the closed season shall be between December 16 and September 7.

In South Dakota the closed season shall be between December 16 and September 10.

In New York, other than on Long Island, and in Oregon the closed season shall be between December 16 and September 16.

In New Hampshire, Long Island, New Jersey, and Washington the closed season shall be between January 16 and October 1.

Rails.—The closed season on rails, coots, and gallinules shall be between December 1 and September 1 next following, except as follows:

Exceptions: In Massachusetts and Rhode Island the closed season shall be between December 1 and August 1.

In New York and on Long Island the closed season shall be between December 1 and September 16; and

On rails in California and Vermont the closed season shall be until September 1, 1918.

Woodcock.—The closed season on woodcock shall be between December 1 and October 1 next following, except as follows:

Exceptions: In Maine and Vermont the closed season shall be between December 1 and September 15.

In Massachusetts, Connecticut, and New Jersey the closed season shall be between December 1 and October 10.

In Rhode Island, Pennsylvania, and on Long Island the closed season shall be between December 1 and October 15; and

In Illinois and Missouri the closed season shall be until September 1, 1918.

Shore birds.—The closed season on black-breasted and golden plover, jacksnipe or Wilson snipe, and greater or lesser yellowlegs shall be between December 16 and September 1 next following, except as follows:

Exceptions: In Maine, Massachusetts, and on Long Island the closed season shall be between December 16 and August 1.

In Minnesota and North Dakota the closed season shall be between December 16 and September 7.

In South Dakota the closed season shall be between December 16 and September 10.

In New York, other than Long Island, and in Oregon the closed season shall be between December 16 and September 16; and

In New Hampshire and Washington the closed season shall be between December 16 and October 1.

Regulation 9. Closed Seasons in Zone No. 2.

Closed seasons in zone No. 2 shall be as follows:

Waterfowl.—The closed season on waterfowl shall be between January 16 and October 1 next following, except as follows:

Exceptions: In Kansas, Oklahoma, New Mexico, and Arizona the closed season shall be between December 16 and September 1; and

In Maryland, Virginia, North Carolina, and South Carolina the closed season shall be between February 1 and November 1.

Rails.—The closed season on rails, coots, and gallinules shall be between December 1 and September 1 next following, except as follows:

Exceptions: In Tennessee and Louisiana the closed season shall be between December 1 and October 1; and

In Arizona the closed season shall be between December 1 and October 15.

Woodcock.—The closed season on woodcock shall be between January 1 and November 1, except as follows:

Exceptions: In Louisiana the closed season shall be between January 1 and November 15; and

In Georgia the closed season shall be between January 1 and December 1.

Shore birds.—The closed season on black-breasted and golden plover, jacksnipe or Wilson snipe, and greater and lesser yellowlegs shall be between December 16 and September 1, next following, except as follows:

Exceptions: In Alabama the closed season shall be between December 16 and November 1.

In Louisiana and Tennessee the closed season shall be between December 16 and October 1.

In Arizona the closed season shall be between December 16 and October 15.

In Utah, on snipe the closed season shall be between December 16 and October 1, and on plover and yellowlegs shall be until September 1, 1918.

Regulation 10. Hearings.

Persons recommending changes in the regulations or desiring to submit evidence in person or by attorney as to the necessity for such changes should make application to the Secretary of Agriculture. Whenever possible hearings will be arranged at central points, and due notice thereof given by publication or otherwise as may be deemed appropriate. Persons recommending changes should be prepared to show the necessity for such action and to submit evidence other than that based on reasons of personal convenience or a desire to kill game during a longer open season.

OPEN SEASONS.

All the general open seasons for game prescribed by the various States and by the Provinces of Canada are here brought together in one table. For the sake of simplicity a uniform method is used in both the arrangement of species and statement of seasons. In each case deer and other big game are first considered; then rabbits and squirrels; then upland game birds, such as quail, grouse, pheasants, turkeys, and doves; then shore birds; and finally waterfowl, such as ducks, geese, and swans. In stating the seasons the plan of the Vermont law, to include the first date but not the last, has been followed consistently.[1] The Vermont scheme has the advantage of showing readily both the open and close seasons, since either may be obtained by reversing the dates of the other.

In some States certain days of the week constitute close seasons throughout the time in which killing is permitted. Hunting on Sunday is prohibited in all of the States and Provinces east of the one hundred and fifth meridian except Illinois, Louisiana, Michigan, Texas, Wisconsin, and Quebec. Mondays constitute a close season for waterfowl in Ohio, and locally in Maryland and North Carolina; and other week days for wild fowl in several favorite ducking grounds in Delaware, Maryland, Virginia, and North Carolina. Hunting is prohibited on election day in Allegany, Baltimore, Cecil, Frederick, and Harford Counties, Md.; and when snow is on the ground in New Jersey, Delaware, Virginia, and Maryland. The county laws of Maryland and North Carolina, which are too numerous to be included satisfactorily, are not incorporated in the following table,[2] which otherwise may be regarded as a practically complete résumé of the regulations now in force. The difficulty of securing absolute accuracy in a table of this kind is very great, and the absence in the laws of many States of express legislation as to the inclusion or exclusion of the date upon which seasons open and close makes exactness almost an impossibility.

In the following table all dates in black-faced type are in accordance with the proposed regulations for the protection of migratory birds, which do not take effect until October 1 or on approval by the President. As these regulations have not yet been approved, the opening date of the season for 1913 under State laws has been indicated. *Names of birds in black-faced type* indicate in most cases that these species are protected only by the Federal law. Species like the curlew, upland plover, swan, the smaller shore birds, and the wood duck in Zone No. 1, which will be protected for five years under the proposed regulations are not included in the table unless mentioned in the State law.

All seasons for migratory birds are necessarily provisional and subject to change when the regulations take effect.

---

[1] See discussion of this question in Circular No. 43 of the Biological Survey, U. S. Department of Agriculture, 1904, entitled "Definitions of the open and close seasons for game."

[2] The county laws of Maryland are shown in Poster No. 28, and those of North Carolina in Poster No. 30, copies of which may be had free on application to the Biological Survey, U. S. Department of Agriculture.

PROVISIONAL OPEN SEASONS FOR GAME IN THE UNITED STATES AND CANADA, 1913.

[The open seasons include the first date, but not the last. To find the close seasons, *reverse the dates.* Seasons which apply only to special counties are placed to the left of the column containing those for the State in general. Future dates, as Aug. 1, 1914, indicate that the season does not open until that time.]

Alabama (1907-1911): *Open seasons.*

- Male deer (does protected all the year) .... Nov. 1-Jan. 1.
- Squirrel (black, gray, or fox) .... Oct. 1-Mar. 1.
- Quail or partridge .... Nov. 1-Mar. 1.
- Wild turkey gobblers (hens protected all the year) .... Dec. 1-Apr. 1.
- Ruffed grouse (pheasant), imported pheasant, or other introduced game birds .... Dec. 1-Dec. 15.
- Dove .... Aug. 1-Mar. 1.
- Plover, snipe .... Nov. 1-**Dec. 16.**
- Yellowlegs .... Sept. 1-**Dec. 16.**
- Curlew, sandpiper, other shore birds, swan .... Sept. 1-Mar. 15.
- Woodcock .... Sept. 1-**Jan. 1.**
- Rail, coot, mud hens .... Sept. 1-**Dec. 1.**
- Duck, goose, brant .... Sept. 1-**Jan. 16.**

Alaska[1] (1910-1913):

North of latitude 62°—

- Moose (females and yearlings protected all the year), caribou, sheep .... Aug. 1-Dec. 11.

South of latitude 62°—

- Deer (see exception) .... Aug. 15-Nov. 2.
  - *Exception:* Deer on Duke, Gravina, Kruzof, Suemez, and Zarembo Islands, Aug. 1, 1914; Kodiak and Long Islands, Dec. 10, 1914.
- Mountain goat .... Aug. 1-Feb. 2.
- Moose (females and yearlings protected all the year), caribou (see exception), sheep .... Aug. 20-Jan. 1.
  - *Exception:* Caribou on the Kenai Peninsula, Aug. 1, 1914.
- Brown bear .... Oct. 1-July 2.

Throughout Territory—

- Grouse, ptarmigan, shore birds, waterfowl .... Sept. 1-Mar. 2.

Arizona (1912):

- Male deer .... Oct. 1-Dec. 16.
- Female deer, spotted fawn, elk, antelope, sheep, goat .... No open season.
- Bobwhite, grouse, pheasant .... No open season.
- Quail .... Oct. 15-Feb. 2.
- Wild turkey .... Oct. 1-Dec. 16.
- Dove and white wing .... June 1-Feb. 2.
- Duck, goose, and brant .... Sept. 1-**Dec. 16.**
- Snipe, **plover, yellowlegs** .... Oct. 15-**Dec. 16.**
- Rail, **coot, gallinule** .... Oct. 15-**Dec. 1.**

Arkansas (1901-1913):

- Deer (see exceptions) .... Sept. 1-Feb. 1.
  - *Exceptions:*
    - Chicot County .... Oct. 1-Feb. 1.
    - Desha County .... Oct. 1-Jan. 1.
- Squirrel in Lee, Monroe, Phillips, and St. Francis Counties .... May 1-Dec. 1.
- Quail or partridge (see exceptions) .... Nov. 1-Mar. 1.
  - *Exceptions:*
    - Bradley and Dallas Counties .... Nov. 15-Mar. 1.
    - Carroll, Columbia, Grant, and Lafayette Counties .... Dec. 10-Feb. 1.
    - Boone County, quail .... Mar. 29, 1917.
    - Calhoun county, nonresident not permitted to hunt quail or partridge.
- Prairie chicken, pinnated grouse (see exception) .... Nov. 1-Dec. 1.
  - *Exception:* Prairie County .... Jan. 1, 1917.
- Wild turkey (see exception) .... Sept. 1-May 1.
  - *Exception:* Chicot County .... Feb. 1-May 15.
- Pheasants (Chinese, English) 10 years .... Mar. 14, 1913.
- Dove .... No open season.
- **Black-breasted and golden plover, jacksnipe, Wilson snipe, and yellowlegs**[2] .... **Sept. 1-Dec. 16.**
- **Woodcock** .... **Nov. 1-Jan. 1.**
- **Rail, coot, gallinule** .... **Sept. 1-Dec. 1.**
- **Duck, goose, brant** .... **Oct. 1-Jan. 16.**

---

[1] Game animals or birds may be killed at any time for food or clothing by native Indians or Eskimo, or by miners or explorers in need of food, but game so killed can not be shipped or sold.

[2] See Regulation 4.

	Open seasons.
California (1901–1913):[1]	
Male deer in second, fourth, and fifth districts	July 1–Sept. 1.
In first, third, and seventh districts	Aug. 15–Nov. 1.
In sixth district	Aug. 15–Sept. 15.
Female deer, fawn, elk, antelope, sheep	No open season.
Cottontail rabbit, bush rabbit	July 31–Feb. 1.
Tree squirrel (except in Mendocino County, unprotected)	Sept. 1–Jan. 1.
Valley quail (except sixth district, Oct. 15–Nov. 15)	Oct. 15–Feb. 15.
Mountain quail, grouse, sage hen	Sept. 1–Dec. 1.
Pheasant, bobwhite quail, imported quail or partridge, wild turkey, swan	No open season.
Dove	July 15–Oct. 1.
In second and fifth districts	Aug. 1–Oct. 15.
In fourth and sixth districts and Inyo County of the seventh district	Sept. 1–Nov. 1.
Black-breasted and golden plover, Wilson or jacksnipe	Nov. 15–**Dec. 16.**
Rail, band tailed pigeon (Regulations Nos. 4 and 8)	**Sept. 1, 1918.**
Duck	Oct. 15–**Jan. 16.**
Black brant (opens Oct. 1 in first district)	Nov. 1–**Jan. 16.**
Colorado (1899–1913):	
Deer with horns	Oct. 1, 1918.
Elk, 15 years	Nov. 1, 1924.
Antelope, 13 years; sheep with horns, 15 years	Sept. 25, 1924.
Deer, antelope, sheep, without horns	No open season.
Partridge, ptarmigan, wild turkey, wild pigeon	No open season.
Quail (bobwhite, crested), 13 years	Oct. 1, 1924.
Pheasant, black game, capercailzie	Sept. 1, 1924.
Prairie chicken, mountain and willow grouse	Aug. 15–Oct. 11.
Sage chicken	Sept. 1–Apr. 21.
Dove	Aug. 15–Sept. 1.
Plover, snipe	Sept. 1–**Dec. 16.**
Yellowlegs	Aug. 1–**Dec. 16.**
Curlew (under Regulation No. 4)	**Sept. 1, 1918.**
Rails, coots, gallinules	**Sept. 1–Dec. 1.**
Duck, goose, brant	Sept. 1–**Dec. 16.**
Connecticut (1901–1913):	
Deer, 6 years	June 1, 1917.
Hare, rabbit	Oct. 8–Jan. 1.[2]
Gray squirrel	Oct. 8–Nov. 24.
Quail, ruffed grouse, pheasant (Chinese, English, Mongolian), woodcock	Oct. 8–Nov. 24.
Hungarian partridge	Nov. 1–24, 1913.
Dove	No open season.
Black-breasted and golden plover, Wilson or English snipe, yellowlegs, duck (except wood duck; Sept. 1, 1919), goose, brant	Sept. 1–**Dec. 16.**
Rail	Sept. 12–**Dec. 1.**
Mud-hen, gallinule	Sept. 1–**Dec. 1.**
Delaware (1893–1913):	
Rabbit, hare, squirrel (fox, black, gray)	Nov. 15–Jan. 1.
Quail, partridge, woodcock	Nov. 15–Jan. 1.
Hungarian partridge, pheasant, swan	No open season.
Dove (except in Newcastle County, no open season)	Aug. 1–Jan. 1.
Reedbird, ortolan, or rail	Sept. 1–Nov. 1.
Duck (except wood duck, Sept. 1–Nov. 1), goose, brant	**Oct. 1–Jan. 16.**
Black-breasted and golden plover, jacksnipe or Wilson snipe, yellowlegs	**Sept. 1–Dec. 16.**

[1] Seasons fixed by ordinances of boards of county supervisors are omitted. The following seven fish and game districts have been established in California: *First district:* Northern counties, including Siskiyou, Modoc, Lassen, Shasta, Trinity, Tehama. *Second district:* Coast counties north of Suisun Bay and west of the Sacramento River, including Del Norte, Humboldt, Mendocino, Glenn, Colusa, Lake, Sonoma, Napa, Yolo, Solano, Marin. *Third district:* Counties of the eastern Sacramento Valley and central Sierra, including Plumas, Butte, Sierra, Yuba, Sutter, Nevada, Placer, El Dorado, Sacramento, Amador, Calaveras, San Joaquin, Tuolumne, Mariposa. *Fourth district:* San Joaquin Valley counties, including Madera, Tulare, and east of the San Joaquin River in Stanislaus, Merced, Fresno, Kings, Kern. *Fifth district:* Counties west of the Coast Range from Suisun Bay to Santa Barbara, including Contra Costa, Alameda, San Francisco, San Mateo, Santa Clara, Santa Cruz, San Benito, Monterey, San Luis Obispo, Santa Barbara, and west of San Joaquin River in Stanislaus, Merced, Fresno, Kings, and Kern counties. *Sixth district:* Southern California, including counties of Ventura, Los Angeles, Orange, San Diego, Imperial, Riverside, and San Bernardino. *Seventh district:* Central counties east of the Sierra, including Alpine, Mono, and Inyo.

[2] Between Nov. 24 and Jan. 1 hunting is permitted with dog and ferret only.

	Open seasons.
District of Columbia [1] (1899–1906):	
Deer meat (sale or possession)	Sept. 1–Jan. 1.
Rabbit (except English rabbit, Belgian hare), squirrel	Nov. 1–Feb. 1.
Quail or partridge	Nov. 1–Mar. 15.
Ruffed grouse or pheasant (except English, ringneck, or other imported pheasants raised in inclosures, sale or possession unrestricted), wild turkey	Nov. 1–Dec. 26.
Prairie chicken (pinnated grouse)	Sept. 1–Mar. 15.
Dove	No open season.
Woodcock	July 1–Jan. 1.
Plover, snipe, marsh blackbird, duck, goose, brant	Sept. 1–**Dec. 16.**
Reedbird	Sept. 1–**Nov. 1.**
Rail or ortolan	**Sept. 1.**–Dec. 1.
Florida (1913):	
Deer, males only (does and fawns, no open season), squirrel	Nov. 20–Feb. 21.
Quail (bobwhite partridge), wild turkey gobblers (hens, no open season), dove	Nov. 20–Feb. 21.
Ruffed grouse, imported pheasants	Dec. 1, 1915.
Plover, snipe, **yellowlegs**	Nov. 20–**Dec. 16.**
Rail, coot, **gallinule**	Nov. 20–**Dec. 1.**
Duck, goose, brant	Nov. 20–**Jan. 16.**
Georgia (1905–1912):	
Deer (except does and fawns, Dec. 1, 1916)	Oct. 1–Dec. 1.
Cat squirrel (fox squirrel, Jan. 1, 1918)	Aug. 1–Jan. 1.
Quail, partridge, wild turkey (gobblers), dove	Nov. 20–Mar. 1.
Pheasant or ruffed grouse, wild turkey hens, imported game birds	Dec. 1, 1916.
Plover	Nov. 20–**Dec. 16.**
Snipe	Dec. 1–**Dec. 16.**
Yellowlegs	**Sept. 1–Dec. 16.**
Woodcock	Dec. 1–Jan. 1.
Rail, coot, gallinule	**Sept. 1–Dec. 1.**
Ducks (except wood duck, Dec. 1–Jan. 1)	Sept. 1–**Jan. 16.**
Geese, brant	**Oct. 1–Jan. 16.**
Idaho (1909–1911):	
Deer, elk, sheep, goat (see exceptions)	Sept. 1–Dec. 1.
Exceptions.—In Bonner, Clearwater, Idaho, Kootenai, Latah, Nez Perce, and Shoshone Counties, deer, Sept. 20–Dec. 20; elk, Sept. 1, 1916; in Fremont, Bonneville, and Bingham Counties, elk, Sept. 1–Jan. 1; in Bear Lake, Cassia, Oneida, and Twinfalls Counties, deer, elk, sheep, and goat, Sept. 1, 1916.	
Moose, caribou, antelope, buffalo	No open season.
Quail	Nov. 1–Dec. 1.
Partridge, pheasant, grouse (except north of Salmon River, Sept. 1–Dec. 1)	Aug. 15–Dec. 1.
Turtle dove (except in Fremont County, Aug. 15–Dec. 1), sage hen	July 15–Dec. 1.
Prairie chicken, pinnated grouse, imported pheasant	No open season.
Swan	Sept. 1, **1918.**
Plover, snipe, yellowlegs	Sept. 1–**Dec. 16.**
Duck, goose, **brant**	Sept. 1–**Dec. 16.**
Rail, coot, gallinule	**Sept. 1–Dec. 1.**
Illinois (1903–1913):	
Deer,[2] 10 years	June 23, 1923.
Squirrel (gray, red, fox, or black)	July 2–Nov. 15.
Quail	Nov. 11–Dec. 10.
Prairie chicken	Nov. 11–Nov. 25.
Ruffed grouse, partridge, blue quail, mountain quail, valley quail, Hungarian partridge, capercailzie, heath hen, black grouse, woodcock	July 2, 1920.
Wild turkey, pheasants [2] (copper or Soemmering, English, golden, green Japanese, Mongolian, ringneck, silver, tragopan, Reeves, Elliot, Hungarian, Swinhoe, Amherst, melanotte, impeyan, argus), partridge (black Indian, caccabis, chukar), sand grouse, 10 years	June 23, 1923.
Mourning dove	Aug. 16–Nov. 1.
Plover, snipe, **yellowlegs,** duck, goose, brant	Sept. 2–**Dec. 16.**
Coot, rail, gallinule	Sept. 2–**Dec. 1.**

[1] Hunting prohibited in the District, by act of June 30, 1906, except on the marshes of the Eastern Branch above the Anacostia Bridge, and on the Virginia shore of the Potomac, and no birds can be shot within 200 yards of any bridge or dwelling.

[2] Deer raised in inclosure for market may be killed Oct. 1–Feb. 1; cock pheasant, Nov. 1–Feb. 1 under permit.

	Open seasons.
Indiana (1905–1913):	
Deer[1]	No open season.
Rabbit	Apr. 1–Jan. 10.
Squirrel	July 1–Oct. 1.
Quail, ruffed grouse	Nov. 10–Dec. 21.
Prairie chicken, Hungarian partridge, pheasants (copper, golden, green, Hungarian, ringneck, silver, tragopan)	Mar. 6, 1915.
Wild turkey, dove	No open season.
Woodcock	July 1–**Dec. 1.**
Black-breasted and golden plover, jacksnipe or Wilson snipe, and yellowlegs	**Sept. 1–Dec. 16.**
Rail, coot, and gallinule	**Sept. 1–Dec. 1.**
Duck, goose, brant	Sept. 1–**Dec. 16.**
Iowa (1897–1907):	
Deer, elk	No open season.
Squirrel (gray, timber, or fox)	Sept. 1–Jan. 1.
Quail, ruffed grouse or pheasant, wild turkey	Nov. 1–Dec. 15.
Prairie chicken (pinnated grouse)	Sept. 1–Dec. 1.
Pheasants (English, Mongolian, Chinese, ringneck)	Oct. 1, 1915.
Turtle dove	No open season.
Woodcock	July 10–**Dec. 1.**
Black-breasted and golden plover, Wilson or jacksnipe, yellowlegs, duck, goose, brant	Sept. 1–**Dec. 16.**
Rail, **coot, gallinule**	Sept. 1–**Dec. 1.**
Kansas (1903–1913):	
Deer, antelope, 10 years	Mar. 24, 1921.
Fox squirrel (red, gray, and black, no open season)	Sept. 1–Jan. 1.
Quail, prairie chicken, pheasants (English, Mongolian, or Chinese), Hungarian partridge, 5 years	Mar. 19, 1918.
Grouse	Oct. 1–Nov. 2.
Plover	Aug. 1–**Dec. 16.**
Snipe, duck, goose, brant	Sept. 1–**Dec. 16.**
Yellowlegs	**Sept. 1–Dec. 16.**
Woodcock	**Nov. 1–Jan. 1.**
Rails, coots, gallinules	**Sept. 1–Dec. 1.**
Kentucky (1894–1906):	
Deer	Sept. 1–Mar. 1.
Rabbit (except with dogs or snares)	Nov. 15–Sept. 15.
Squirrel (black, gray, or fox)	June 15–Sept. 15. Nov. 15–Feb. 1.
Quail, partridge, pheasant	Nov. 15–Jan. 1.
Pheasants (English, ringneck, Mongolian, or Chinese)	No open season.
Wild turkey	Sept. 1–Feb. 1.
Dove	Aug. 1–Feb. 1.
Woodcock	June 20–**Jan. 1.**
Black-breasted and golden plover, Wilson or jacksnipe, yellowlegs	**Sept. 1–Dec. 16.**
Rail, coot, gallinule	**Sept. 1–Dec. 1.**
Duck, goose	Aug. 15–**Jan. 16.**
Brant	**Oct. 1–Jan. 16.**
Louisiana (1912):	
Deer (fawns no open season) 5 months,[2] including	Nov. and Dec.
Squirrels	July 2–Mar. 1.
Quail	Nov. 15–Mar. 1.
Prairie chicken, pheasant (imported or native), wild turkey hen, killdeer	Dec. 1, 1915.
Wild turkey (male)	Nov. 15–Apr. 1.
Dove	Sept. 1–Mar. 1.
Woodcock	Nov. 15–**Jan. 1.**
Papabotte, upland plover (under Regulation No. 4)	**Sept. 1, 1918.**
Plover (except killdeer and upland plover)	Oct. 1–**Dec. 16.**
Snipe	Sept. 15–**Dec. 16.**
Rail, coot, gallinule	Oct. 1–**Dec. 1.**
Duck (except wood duck, black mallard, and blue-winged teal), goose, brant	Oct. 1–**Jan. 16.**
Blue-winged teal	Sept. 15–**Jan. 16.**
Florida duck (black mallard)	Aug. 1–**Jan. 16.**
Wood duck	Sept. 1–**Jan. 16.**

[1] Deer raised in private preserves may be killed at any time.
[2] Season fixed by conservation commission.

Maine (1903–1913):	*Open seasons.*
Deer in Aroostook, Franklin, Hancock, Oxford, Penobscot, Piscataquis, Somerset, and Washington Counties (see exceptions)	Oct. 1–Dec. 16.
Exceptions:	
Mount Desert Island, no open season.	
Swan Island, 4 years — Oct. 1, 1914.	
Washington County—Cross and Scotch Islands — July 3, 1919.	
Deer in rest of State	Nov. 1–Dec. 1.
Bull moose with at least two 3-inch prongs on horns	Nov. 1–Dec. 1.
Cow and calf moose	No open season.
Caribou, 6 years	Oct. 15, 1917.
Hare, rabbit	Sept. 1–Apr. 1.
Squirrel, gray	Sept. 1–Nov. 1.
Quail, Hungarian partridge, pheasant, black game, capercailzie, cock of the woods, dove	No open season.
Ruffed grouse, partridge, woodcock	Sept. 15–Dec. 1.
Plover, snipe, yellowlegs	Aug. 1–Dec. 1.
Rail, coot, gallinule	**Sept. 1–Dec. 1.**
Duck, goose, brant	**Sept. 1–Dec. 16.**
Maryland (1898–1912):[1]	
Rabbit	Nov. 1–Dec. 25.
Squirrel	Sept. 1–Dec. 2.
Quail, ruffed grouse, wild turkey	Nov. 1–Dec. 25.
Dove	Aug. 15–Dec. 25.
Plover, snipe	Aug. 15–**Dec. 16.**
Woodcock	**Nov. 1**–Dec. 25.
Reedbird, sora (water rail or ortolan)	**Sept. 1–Nov. 1.**
Duck, goose, brant	Nov. 1–**Feb. 1.**
Coot and gallinule	**Sept. 1–Dec. 16.**
Yellowlegs	**Sept. 1–Dec. 16.**
Massachusetts (1902–1913):	
Deer (third Monday in November to the following Saturday, inclusive)	Nov. 17–22, 1913.
Moose	No open season.
Hare or rabbit	Oct. 16–Mar. 1.
Gray squirrel	Oct. 12–Nov. 13.
Quail, ruffed grouse or partridge, woodcock	Oct. 12–Nov. 13.
Dove, wild or passenger pigeon, prairie chicken, Hungarian partridge, pheasants (English, golden, Mongolian),[2] killdeer or piping plover, swan	No open season.
Heath hen, 5 years	Nov. 1, 1916.
Wild turkey, 4 years	Sept. 1, 1915.
Bartramian sandpiper (upland plover)	July 15, 1915.
Plover (except upland and killdeer or piping plover), snipe	**Aug. 1–Dec. 16.**
Rail, gallinule, quark (mud hen)	**Aug. 1–Dec. 1.**
Duck (except wood duck), teal, brant	Sept. 15–Jan. 1.
Michigan (1905–1913):	
Deer[3] (see exceptions)	Nov. 10–Dec. 1.
Exceptions: Deer in red coat and fawn in spotted coat, and all deer in Berrien, Calhoun, Genesee, Ingham, Jackson, Kalamazoo, Oakland, and St. Clair Counties	Nov. 10, 1920.
Bois Blanc Island	Nov. 10, 1918.
Elk, moose, caribou	No open season.
Rabbit	Sept. 1–Mar. 2.
Squirrel (black, fox, or gray), 3 years	Oct. 15, 1915.
Quail, pheasants (English, Mongolian), black game, capercailzie, hazel grouse, wild turkey	Nov. 1, 1917.
Ruffed grouse (partridge), spruce hen, woodcock	Oct. 1–Dec. 1.
Pinnated grouse (prairie chicken), European partridge, dove, swan	No open season.
Plover, snipe, **yellowlegs,** duck, goose, brant	Sept. 1–**Dec. 16.**
Rail, coot, **gallinule**	Sept. 15–**Dec. 1.**

[1] The seasons given are the most general. For all seasons under county laws see Poster No. 28, "Open seasons for game, District of Columbia, Maryland, and Virginia, 1913," which may be had upon application to the Biological Survey, U. S. Department of Agriculture, Washington, D. C.

[2] Except on private preserves under permit of commissioners on fisheries and game.

[3] Deer raised in captivity may be killed at any time for owner's consumption.

	Open seasons.
Minnesota (1905–1909):	
Deer, male moose	Nov. 10–Nov. 30.
Elk, female moose, caribou, fawn	No open season.
Quail, partridge, ruffed grouse (pheasant)	Oct. 1–Dec. 1.
Sharp-tailed or white-breasted grouse, prairie chicken (pinnated grouse), turtle dove, golden plover, Wilson or jack snipe, woodcock	Sept. 7–Nov. 7.
Pheasants (Chinese, English, Mongolian)	No open season.
Duck, goose, brant	Sept. 7–Dec. 1.
Rail, coot, gallinule	**Sept. 1–Dec. 1.**
Mississippi[1] (1906–1910):	
Deer (female deer and spotted fawn, no open season), bear	Nov. 15–Mar. 1.
Quail or partridge	Nov. 1–Mar. 1.
Wild turkey (hens, no open season)	Jan. 1–May 1.
Dove	July 1–Mar. 1.
Plover, tatler, chorook, grosbec, **Jacksnipe or Wilson snipe, and yellowlegs**	Sept. 1–**Dec. 16.**
Coot (poule d'eau), rail (mud hen), **gallinule**	Sept. 1–**Dec. 1.**
Duck, goose, brant	Sept. 1–**Jan. 16.**
Cedar bird	Sept. 1–Mar. 1.
Missouri (1909–1913):	
Deer, males only (no open season for does or fawns under 1 year of age)	Nov. 1–Jan. 1.
Squirrel (gray, black, fox)	July 1–Dec. 1.
Quail (bobwhite, partridge)	Dec. 1–Jan. 1.
Wild turkey	Nov. 1–Jan. 1.
Dove	Sept. 1–Jan. 1.
Ruffed grouse (pheasant), prairie chicken (pinnated grouse), Mongolian, Chinese, and English pheasants, woodcock, and other game birds	No open season.
Plover, **yellowlegs**	Sept. 1–**Dec. 16.**
Snipe	Sept. 15–**Dec. 16.**
Rail, coot, gallinule	**Sept. 1–Dec. 1.**
Duck, goose, brant	Sept. 15–**Jan. 16.**
Montana (1905–1913):	
Deer, sheep, goat	Oct. 1–Dec. 1.
Elk (see exceptions)	Oct. 1, 1918.
Exceptions: In counties of Sweetgrass, Park, Gallatin, Madison, Teton, Flathead, and those portions of Powell and Missoula Counties drained by South Fork of Flathead and Swan Rivers, respectively, Beaverhead County east of Oregon Short Line Railroad between Willis and Armstead, and Beaverhead County south of Pittsburg and Gilmore Railroad	Oct. 1–Dec. 1.
Moose, caribou, fawns, female sheep, and lambs, antelope, bison or buffalo	No open season.
Quail, Chinese pheasant, Hungarian pheasant, dove	No open season.
Pheasant, partridge, prairie chicken, sage hen, fool hen, grouse	Oct. 1–Nov. 1.
Duck, goose, brant	Sept. 1–**Dec. 16.**
Black-breasted and golden plover, jacksnipe or Wilson snipe, and yellowlegs	**Sept. 1–Dec. 16.**
Rail, coot, gallinule	**Sept. 1–Dec. 1.**
Nebraska (1901–1911):	
Deer, elk, antelope	No open season.
Squirrel (gray, red, fox, timber)	Oct. 1–Dec. 1.
Quail	Nov. 1–Nov. 16.
Dove, plover (except killdeer)	July 15–Sept. 1.
Prairie chicken, sage chicken, grouse	Sept. 1–Dec. 1.
Partridge, pheasant, ptarmigan, English partridge, Belgian partridge, English pheasant, Chinese pheasant, Mongolian pheasant, English black cock, other imported game birds, wild pigeon, wild turkey, curlew, white crane, swan	No open season.
Yellowlegs, jacksnipe, Wilson snipe, duck, goose, brant	Sept. 1–**Dec. 16.**
Rail, coot, and gallinule	**Sept. 1–Dec. 1.**
Nevada[2] (1909–1913):	
Deer (males only)	Oct. 15–Nov. 16.
Antelope, female deer, spotted fawn	No open season.
Mountain sheep and goat	Jan. 1, 1920.
Mountain quail	Oct. 1–Jan. 2.
Valley quail	Oct. 15–Jan. 16.
Grouse	Oct. 1–Dec 16.

[1] Local regulations of boards of supervisors also in force.

[2] County commissioners may change dates of close seasons (without altering length) and may open seasons for shorebirds and waterfowl Sept. 1.

	Open seasons.
Nevada—Continued.	
Bobwhite, partridge, pheasant, other imported birds	No open season.
Sage hen	July 15–Oct. 2.
Woodcock	Sept. 15–**Jan. 1.**
Plover, snipe	Sept. 15–**Dec. 16.**
Duck, goose, swan	Sept. 15–**Jan. 16.**
Brant	**Oct. 1–Jan. 16.**
Yellowlegs	**Sept. 1–Dec. 16.**
New Hampshire [1] (1901–1913):	
Deer in Coos County	Oct. 1–Dec. 16
Deer in Carroll and Grafton Counties	Nov. 1–Dec. 16
Deer in rest of State	Dec. 1–Dec. 16.
Elk, moose, caribou	No open season.
Hare, rabbit	Oct. 1–Apr. 1.
Gray squirrel	Oct. 1, 1919.
Exception: Outside of the thickly settled part of cities and towns	Oct. 1–Nov. 1
Quail, partridge, ruffed grouse, woodcock (see exception), Wilson snipe	Oct. 1–Dec. 1.
Exception: Woodcock in Coos and Grafton Counties	Sept. 15–Dec. 1
Dove, pheasant, any introduced foreign game bird	No open season.
Killdeer, upland plover or Bartramian sandpiper, wood duck	Oct. 1, 1917.
Black-breasted and golden plover, yellowlegs	Oct. 1–**Dec. 16.**[2]
Rail, **coot, gallinule**	**Sept. 1–Dec. 1.**[2]
Duck (except wood duck and sheldrake), **goose, brant**	Oct. 1–**Jan. 16.**[3]
New Jersey (1903–1913):	
Deer, bucks only [4] (no open season for does)	Nov. 1–Nov. 6.
Rabbit, squirrel	Nov. 10–Dec. 16.
Quail, ruffed grouse (partridge), prairie chicken, Hungarian partridge, English or ring-neck pheasant (females until 1914), wild turkey	Nov. 10–Dec. 16.
Dove, wild pigeon	No open season.
Woodcock	Oct. 10–Dec. 1.
Upland plover, 5 years	Aug. 1, 1916.
Plover (except upland plover), yellowlegs	May 1–**Dec. 16.**
English (Wilson) snipe (bog or jacksnipe)	Sept. 1–**Dec. 16.**
Curlew, surf (bay) snipe (except English snipe), sandpiper, and other shore birds	May 1–Jan. 1.
Reedbird	Sept. 1–**Nov. 1.**
Marsh hen, rail, **coot, gallinule**	Sept. 1–**Dec. 1.**
Duck (except wood duck, swan, **Sept. 1, 1918**), goose, brant	Nov. 1–**Jan. 16.**[5]
New Mexico (1912):	
Deer (with horns)	Oct. 1–Nov. 16.
Deer (without horns), **elk, sheep, goat**	No open season.
Antelope, 5 years	June 14, 1917.
Quail (except bobwhite)	Nov. 1–Feb. 1.
Bobwhite quail, pheasant, prairie chicken, wild pigeon, 5 years	June 14, 1917.
Grouse	Sept. 1–Nov. 16.
Ptarmigan (white grouse), Oregon or Denny pheasant	No open season.
Wild turkey	Nov. 1–Jan. 16.
Turtle dove	July 1–Oct. 1.
Plover, snipe, **yellowlegs,** duck, **goose, brant**	Sept. 1–**Dec. 16.**
Rail, coot, gallinule	**Sept. 1–Dec. 1.**
New York [6] (1912–13):	
Deer, with horns not less than 3 inches long, in Adirondack region [7]	Oct. 1–Nov. 16.
Deer—rest of State (see exception)	No open season.
Exception: Deer having horns not less than 3 inches in length in Ulster County and towns of Neversink, Cochecton, Tusten, Highland, Lumberland, Forestburg, Bethel, and all of towns of Mamakating and Thompson south of Newburgh and Cochecton turnpike in Sullivan County and Deer Park in Orange County	Nov. 1–Nov. 16

[1] Governor and council may suspend open season in time of excessive drought.

[2] In Rockingham County the season on beach birds, coot, teal, opens July 15.

[3] On tide waters and salt marshes the season on black ducks opens September 1.

[4] Not applicable to deer in game preserves or to possession of imported deer properly tagged.

[5] Open season for duck, goose, and brant on Delaware River and Bay, begins Sept. 1.

[6] When first date of open season falls on Sunday, season opens on the preceding Saturday.

[7] The Adirondack region comprises the counties of Clinton, Essex, Franklin, Fulton, Hamilton, Herkimer, Oswego, Saratoga, St. Lawrence, Warren, and Washington, and that part of Jefferson, Lewis, and Oneida Counties lying east of the Utica & Black River R. R. from Utica to Ogdensburg.

	Open seasons.
New York—Continued.	
Elk, moose, caribou, antelope, female deer, and fawns	No open season.
Varying hare, rabbit	Oct. 1–Feb. 1.
Squirrel, black, gray, or fox	Oct. 1–Nov. 16.
Quail	Oct. 1, 1918.
Woodcock	Oct. 1–Nov. 16.
Grouse, partridge	Oct. 1–Dec. 1.
Hungarian or European gray-legged partridge, dove, wood duck, swan	No open season.
Wild pheasants, males only	Oct. 2, 9, 16, 23, 30[1]
Plover, snipe	Sept. 16–Dec. 1.
Rail, coot, mud hen, gallinule	**Sept. 16–Dec. 1.**
Waterfowl (except wood duck and swan)	**Sept. 16–Dec. 16.**
Long Island (1912–1913):	
Deer	No open season.
Varying hare, rabbit (cottontail)	Nov. 1–Jan. 1.
Squirrel, black, gray, fox	Nov. 1–Jan. 1.
Quail, pheasants (males only), grouse	Nov. 1–Jan. 1.
Dove	No open season.
Woodcock	Oct. 15–Dec. 1.
Plover, snipe	Aug. 1–Dec. 1.
Rail, coot, mud hen, gallinule	**Sept. 16–Dec. 1.**
Waterfowl (except wood duck and swan no open season)	Oct. 1–Jan. 11.
North Carolina[2] (1905–1911):	
Deer	Oct. 1–Feb. 1.
Quail, wild turkey, dove	Nov. 1–Mar. 1.
Black-breasted and golden plover, jacksnipe or Wilson snipe, yellowlegs	**Sept. 1–Dec.**
Woodcock	**Nov. 1–Jan. 1.**
Rail, coot, gallinule	**Sept. 1–Dec. 1.**
Duck, goose, brant	**Nov. 1–Feb. 1.**
North Dakota (1909–1913):	
Deer, 3 years	Nov. 10, 1916.
Antelope, 11 years	Jan. 1, 1920.
Quail, partridge, English pheasant, Chinese ringneck pheasant, Hungarian partridge, dove, swan	No open season.
Prairie chicken (pinnated grouse), sharp-tailed (white-breasted) grouse, woodcock, golden plover, snipe	Sept. 7–Nov. 2.
Duck, goose, brant	Sept. 7–Dec. 16.
Rail, coot, gallinule	**Sept. 1–Dec. 1.**
Ohio (1900–1913):	
Rabbit	Nov. 15–Dec. 5.
Squirrel	Sept. 15–Oct. 21.
Raccoon	Nov. 1–Mar. 2.
Quail, ruffed grouse, introduced pheasant, dove	Nov. 15, 1915.
Woodcock, coot or mud hen, rail, gallinule	**Sept. 1–Dec. 1.**
Plover, snipe, shore birds, duck, goose, swan	**Sept. 1–Dec. 2.**[3]
Oklahoma (1909–1913):	
Deer (except females throughout State and males in Caddo, Comanche, Kiowa, and Swanson Counties, no open season)	Nov. 15–Dec. 15
Antelope, 5 years	Nov. 15, 1916.
Quail, Mexican (blue) quail	Nov. 15–Feb. 1.
Wild pigeon	No open season.
Prairie chicken	Sept. 1–Nov. 1.
Mongolian, Chinese, English, ringneck, or other pheasant	Nov. 1, 1914.
Wild turkey (additional season for gobblers, Mar. 15–Apr. 15)	Nov. 15–Jan. 1.
Dove	Aug. 15–May 1.
Black-breasted and golden plover, Wilson snipe, or jacksnipe, yellowlegs	**Aug. 15–Dec. 16.**
Rail, coot, gallinule	**Sept. 1–Dec. 1.**
Duck, goose, brant	**Aug. 15–Dec. 16.**

[1] Pheasants are protected by order of the commission until October 1, 1914, in the 17 counties of Chenango, Clinton, Delaware, Essex, Franklin, Fulton, Herkimer, Jefferson, Lewis, Madison, Montgomery, Oneida, Otsego, Saint Lawrence, Schenectady, Warren, and Washington; and until October 1, 1915, in the three counties of Allegany, Cattaraugus, and Chautauqua.

[2] For county seasons see special poster of the Biological Survey, U. S. Department of Agriculture.

[3] Sundays and Mondays are close seasons for ducks and other waterfowl.

	Open seasons.
Oregon (1909–1913):	
District No. 1.[1]—	
Male deer	Aug. 1–Nov. 1.
Female deer and spotted fawn, moose, elk, antelope, caribou, sheep, goat	No open season.
Silver gray squirrel	Oct. 1–Nov. 1.
Quail, grouse, male Chinese pheasant (except in Coos, Curry, Jackson, and Josephine Counties, no open season)	Oct. 1–Nov. 1.
Pheasant (silver, golden, Reeves, and English), Hungarian partridge, bobwhite, prairie chicken, Franklin grouse, foolhen, wild turkey, plover (semipalmated, snowy), sandpiper (Least, western, solitary), and swan	No open season.
Dove, wild pigeon	Sept. 1–Nov. 1.
Plover, snipe, yellowlegs	**Nov. 1–Dec. 16.**[2]
Rail, coot, gallinule	**Nov. 1–Dec. 1.**[2]
Duck, goose[3]	**Nov. 1–Dec. 16.**[2]
Brant	**Sept.16–Dec.16.**
District No. 2.—Open seasons same as in district No. 1, except as follows:	
Silver gray squirrel	No open season.
Quail, pheasant	No open season.
Dove	Sept. 1–Nov. 1.
Ruffed grouse, native pheasant, blue or sooty grouse	Sept. 1–Nov. 1.
Sage hen	Aug. 1–Sept. 1.
Black-breasted and golden plover, jacksnipe or Wilson snipe, yellowlegs, duck, goose	**Sept.15–Dec.16.**
Rail, coot	**Sept. 15–Dec. 1.**
Pennsylvania (1909–1913):[4]	
Deer—male with horns 2 inches above the hair	Nov. 10–26.
Elk	Nov. 15, 1921.
Bear	Oct. 1–Jan. 1.
Hare, rabbit	Nov. 1–Jan. 1.
Squirrel (gray, black, fox)	Oct. 15–Dec. 1.
Raccoon	Sept. 1–Jan. 1.
Quail	Nov. 1–Dec. 16.
Ruffed grouse, imported pheasants (Chinese, English), Hungarian partridge, woodcock	Oct. 15–Dec. 1.
Wild turkey	May 8, 1915.
Dove, blackbird, killdeer plover	No open season.
Black-breasted and golden plover, jacksnipe or Wilson snipe, yellowlegs	**Sept. 1–Dec. 16.**
Upland or grass plover, reedbird (Federal Regulations Nos. 3 and 4)	**Sept. 1, 1918.**
Rail, coot, mud hen, gallinule	**Sept. 1–Dec. 1.**
Wild waterfowl—duck, goose, brant, loon, grebe	**Sept. 1–Dec.16.**
Rhode Island (1900–1913):	
Deer[5]	No open season.
Gray squirrel, hare, rabbit	Nov. 1–Jan. 1.
Quail or bobwhite, ruffed grouse or partridge	Nov. 1–Jan. 1.
Dove	No open season.
Pheasant, Hungarian partridge	Oct. 15, 1920.
Woodcock	Nov. 1–**Dec. 1.**
Plover, yellowlegs, snipe	July 15–Dec. 16.
Duck, goose, brant	Aug. 15–**Dec. 16.**
Rail, coot, gallinule	**Aug. 1–Dec. 1.**
South Carolina (1902–1912):	
Deer (except Berkeley County, Aug. 1–Feb. 1)	Sept. 1–Jan. 1.
Quail (partridge), wild turkey (except Berkeley County, Nov. 1–Apr. 1)	Nov. 15–Mar. 15.
Dove	Aug. 15–Mar. 1.
Woodcock	**Sept. 1–Jan. 1.**
Wood duck	**Sept. 1–Feb. 1.**

[1] District No. 1, west of Cascades, includes Benton, Clackamas, Clatsop, Columbia, Coos, Curry, Douglas, Jackson, Josephine, Lane, Lincoln, Linn, Marion, Multnomah, Polk, Tillamook, Washington, Yamhil. Counties. District No. 2, east of Cascades, includes the other counties in the State.

[2] In Clatsop, Columbia, Coos, Multnomah, and Tillamook Counties the season opens Sept. 15.

[3] Unlawful to kill geese at any time on islands or sand bars in the Columbia River east of the Cascades or on Deschutes and John Day Rivers south to junction with White River and Thirtymile Creek, respectively.

[4] Game birds or animals reared in captivity may be killed at any time.

[5] Tame deer kept in confinement may be killed by the owner at any time, or any deer injuring crops, by the owner or occupant of the premises, under permit from secretary of state.

South Carolina—Continued.	*Open seasons.*
Grackle	**Oct. 1–Mar. 1.**
Duck (except wood duck), goose, brant	**Nov. 1–Feb. 1.**
Black-breasted and golden plover, jacksnipe or Wilson snipe, yellowlegs	**Sept. 1–Dec. 16.**
Rail, coot, gallinule	**Sept. 1–Dec. 1.**
South Dakota (1909–1913):	
Deer (except fawns, no open season)	Nov. 1–Dec. 1.
Elk, antelope, mountain sheep	No open season.
Quail, dove	No open season.
Partridge, grouse, prairie chicken, woodcock, golden plover, upland plover, snipe	Sept. 10–Oct. 10.
Introduced pheasant	Jan. 1, 1915.
Ducks, goose, brant, any aquatic fowl	**Sept. 10–Dec. 16.**
Yellowlegs	**Sept. 10–Dec. 16.**
Tennessee (1903–1913):	
Deer (except Fentress County, Dec. 1–Jan. 1)	Oct. 1, 1915.
Squirrel	June 1–Mar. 1.[1]
Quail or partridge (except Haywood County, Dec. 1–Feb. 1; Washington and Unicoi Counties, Mar. 27, 1918)	Nov. 15–Mar. 1.
Grouse, pheasant (except English or ringneck pheasants), wild turkey[2]	Nov. 1–Mar. 1.
Pheasant, English or ringneck	Dec. 1–Jan. 1.
Dove (except in Shelby County, Mar. 1–July 15)	Aug. 1–Apr. 15.
Marsh blackbird	Oct. 1–Apr. 15.
Woodcock	**Oct. 1–Jan. 1.**
Black-breasted and golden plover, Wilson or jacksnipe, yellowlegs	**Oct. 1–Dec. 16.**
Rail, coot, mud-hen	**Oct. 1–Dec. 1.**
Duck (except teal and wood duck, Aug. 1–Jan. 16), goose, brant	**Oct. 1–Jan. 16.**
Texas (1907–1911):	
Deer (female deer and spotted fawn no open season)	Nov. 1–Jan. 1.
Antelope, sheep, 5 years	Nov. 1, 1916.
Quail or partridge, dove	Nov. 1–Feb. 1.
Prairie chicken or pinnated grouse, pheasants (Mongolian, English), 5 years	Nov. 1, 1916.
Wild turkey	Dec. 1–Apr. 1.
Woodcock	**Nov. 1–Jan. 1.**
Black-breasted and golden plover, Wilson or jacksnipe, yellowlegs	**Sept. 1–Dec. 16.**
Rail, coot, gallinule	**Sept. 1–Dec. 1.**
Duck, goose, brant	**Oct. 1–Jan. 16.**
Utah (1909–1913):	
Deer (except in Tooele County Oct. 1, 1918, and except as below)	Oct. 1–Oct. 16.
Exception: Nonresident not permitted to kill deer.	
Elk, antelope, sheep	No open season.
Quail, prairie chicken, pheasants (Chinese, English, Mongolian) dove, robin, shore bird (except snipe), swan (see exceptions)	No open season.
Exceptions: Quail in Garfield, Kane, and Washington Counties .. Sept. 1–Feb. 1	
Quail in Carbon, Davis, Salt Lake, San Pete, Sevier, Uinta, Utah, and Weber Counties .. Oct. 1–Nov. 1	
Iron County .. Oct. 1–Dec. 1.	
Grouse	Oct. 6–Oct. 16.
Sage hen	Aug. 15–Nov. 1.
Black-breasted and golden plover, yellowlegs	**Sept. 1–Dec. 16.**
Snipe	Oct. 1–**Dec.** 16.
Duck, goose	Oct. 1–Jan. 1.
Rail, coot, gallinule	**Sept. 1–Dec. 1.**

[1] *Special squirrel seasons:* Benton, Decatur, Wilson, June 1–Jan. 1; Carroll, June 15–Mar. 1; Carter, July 15–Mar. 1; Crockett, Weakley, July 1–Feb. 1; Dyer, June 1–July 1 and Oct. 1–Jan. 1; Fayette, July 15–Jan. 1; Gibson, Sevier, June 1–Feb. 1; Hardeman, July 15–Feb. 15; Haywood, June 15–Jan. 1; Henderson July 15–Jan. 15; McNairy, Madison, July 1–Mar. 1; Robertson, July 1–Jan. 1; Shelby, June 15–Feb. 1; Stewart, Aug. 1–Feb. 1; Warren, Oct. 1–Mar. 1. Bedford, Blount, Cannon, Clay, Coffee, Cumberland, Dickson, Fentress, Giles, Greene, Hickman, Humphreys, Jackson, Knox, Lawrence, Lincoln, London, Marshall, Maury, Meigs, Moore, Overton, Perry, Pickett, Putnam, Rhea, Sequatchie, Sullivan, Van Buren, Washington, Wayne, White, Williamson, unprotected.

In Chester, Dyer, Hardeman, Hardin, and McNairy Counties anyone may kill squirrels on his own property at any time for his own use.

[2] *Special wild turkey seasons:* Dyer (gobblers), Nov. 1–May 1 (hens), Nov. 1–Feb. 1; Clay, Fentress, Overton, Pickett, Aug. 1–May 1; Lauderdale, Feb. 15, 1915.

	Open seasons.
Vermont[1] (1894–1913):	
Deer with horns not less than 3 inches long[2] (no open season for others)	Nov. 10–Dec. 2.
Moose, caribou	No open season.
Elk, 10 years	Feb. 20, 1923.
Hare, rabbit	Sept. 15–Mar. 1.
Gray squirrel	Sept. 15–Dec. 1.
Quail, ruffed grouse (partridge), woodcock	Sept. 15–Dec. 1.
Pheasant, European partridge, dove, upland plover, wood duck, swan	No open season.
Plover (except upland plover), English snipe, yellowlegs	Sept. 1–Dec. 1.
Duck (except wood duck), goose, brant	**Sept. 1–Dec. 16.**
Coot, gallinule	**Sept. 1–Dec. 1.**
Virginia[3] (1903–1912):	
Deer (except in Brunswick and Greenesville Counties, Oct. 1–Feb. 1)	Sept. 1–Dec. 1.
Rabbit	Nov. 1–Feb. 1.[4]
Squirrel:	
Brunswick and Greenesville Counties — Nov. 1–Feb. 1[5]	
Isle of Wight and Southampton Counties (gray or fox) — Sept. 1–Jan. 15	
Warren County — Nov. 15–Jan. 1	
Opossum in Halifax County	Oct. 15–Feb. 1
Quail or partridge, pheasant or grouse, wild turkey (see exception)	Nov. 1–Feb. 1.
Exception: West of the Blue Ridge — Nov. 1–Jan. 1	
Dove in Brunswick and Greenesville Counties	Aug. 15–Jan. 15.
Woodcock	Nov. 1–Jan. 1.
Black-breasted and golden plover	**July 20–Dec. 16.**
Jacksnipe or Wilson snipe, yellowlegs	**Sept. 1–Dec. 16.**
Rail, coot, mud hen, gallinule	**July 20–Dec. 1.**
Summer or wood duck	Aug. 1–Jan. 1.
Winter waterfowl[6] (except in Brunswick and Greenesville Counties, Aug. 1–Jan. 1)	**Oct. 15–Feb. 1.**
Washington[7] (1903–1913):	
Deer (except Okanogan County, Sept. 1–Nov. 1), sheep, goat	Oct. 1–Dec. 1.
Male moose and elk, 12 years	Oct. 1, 1925.
Antelope (males only)	Sept. 15–Nov. 1.
Moose, caribou, spotted fawn, and females of deer, elk, antelope	No open season.
Quail, ruffed grouse, grouse, prairie chicken, pheasant, and other imported upland game birds (see exceptions)	Oct. 1–Dec. 1.
Exceptions:	
East of Cascades, Chinese pheasant (except in Kittitas and Yakima Counties, Oct. 1–16), native pheasant, prairie chicken — Sept. 15–Nov. 1.	
Blue grouse — Sept. 1–Dec. 1.	
Quail east of Cascades (except in Spokane County) — Oct. 1, 1915.	
Western and eastern, prairie chicken, native pheasant, ruffed grouse, Hungarian partridge, bobwhite quail, scaly partridge, sage hen, in Kittitas and Yakima Counties — Oct. 1, 1915.	
California quail in Kittitas and Yakima Counties, Chinese pheasant in Asotin County, and quail, any species of partridge, sage hen, and imported game birds in Okanogan County — Oct. 1, 1915.	
Blue grouse West of Cascades — Sept. 16–Oct. 1.	
Sage grouse, sage hen, band-tailed pigeon, wood duck, and in the counties of Island, King, Pierce, San Juan, Skagit, Snohomish, and Whatcom ruffed grouse — No open season.	
Hungarian partridge	Oct. 1, 1920.
Dove (except east of Cascades, Sept. 15–Nov. 1), swan	No open season.
Blackbreasted and golden plover, jacksnipe or Wilson snipe, yellowlegs	Oct. 1–**Dec. 16.**[8]
Duck, goose, brant	Oct. 1–**Jan. 16.**[8]
Rail	Oct. 1–**Dec. 1.**[8]
Coot and gallinule	**Sept. 1–Dec. 1.**

[1] The governor is authorized to suspend open seasons in time of drought and fix another open season for deer in such event.

[2] Deer kept in private game preserves may be killed by the owners at any time.

[3] Boards of supervisors may shorten the open seasons in their counties and make other restrictions not repugnant to law, "and may include in such protection other game not specifically mentioned in this section." Code 1904, sec. 2070a, as amended in 1906.

[4] Residents of the State may kill rabbits on their own lands at any time.

[5] Residents of State may kill squirrels on their own lands at any time.

[6] Wildfowl can not be hunted on Wednesdays and Saturdays on Back Bay, Princess Anne County.

[7] On Mercer Island and shores of Lake Washington game animals and birds are protected all the year.

[8] The season opens Sept. 15 in Adams, Douglas, Ferry, Grant, Lincoln, Okanogan, Spokane, Stevens, and Whitman Counties.

West Virginia (1909–1913): *Open seasons.*

Deer (with horns more than 4 inches long—no open season for other deer) .... Oct. 15–Dec. 1.
Elk .... 1928.
Squirrel (gray, black, red, fox) .... Sept. 1–Dec. 1.
Quail (Virginia partridge) .... Nov. 1–Dec. 1.
Ruffed grouse (pheasant), wild turkey .... Oct. 15–Dec. 1.
Pheasants (English, Chinese, Reeves, Lady Amherst), capercailzie, or any other introduced foreign game bird, dove, wood duck .... No open season.
Black-breasted and golden plover .... July 15–**Dec. 16.**
Jacksnipe or Wilson snipe .... Oct. 15–**Dec. 16.**
Yellowlegs .... **Sept. 1–Dec. 16**
Woodcock .... July 15–Dec. 20.
Rail (ortolan) .... July 15–**Dec. 1.**
Coot, gallinule .... **Sept. 1–Dec. 1.**
Duck (except wood duck, no open season), goose, brant .... Sept. 1–**Jan. 16.**

Wisconsin (1898–1913):

Deer (see exceptions) .... Nov. 11–Dec. 1.
Exceptions: Wood County, 3 years .... Nov. 10, 1916
Adams, Brown, Buffalo, Calumet, Columbia, Crawford, Dane, Dodge, Door, Fond du Lac, Grant, Green, Green Lake, Iowa, Jefferson, Kenosha, Kewaunee, La Crosse, Lafayette, Manitowoc, Marquette, Milwaukee, Monroe, Outagamie, Ozaukee, Pepin, Portage, Racine, Richland, Rock, Sauk, Sheboygan, Vernon, Walworth, Washington, Waukesha, Waupaca, Waushara, and Winnebago Counties .... No open season
Elk, moose .... No open season.
Rabbit, in Eau Claire, Pierce, Portage, Richland, Vernon, Waupaca, and Waushara Counties .... Sept. 10–Feb. 1.
In Dane, Dunn, Green, Green Lake, Jefferson, Juneau, La Crosse, Outagamie, Marinette, Rock, Trempealeau, Walworth, and Wood Counties .... Oct. 10–Feb. 1.
Squirrel (gray, fox, black, see exceptions) .... Oct. 10–Feb. 1.
Exceptions: Eau Claire, Pierce, Portage, Richland, Vernon, Waupaca, and Waushara Counties .... Sept. 10–Feb. 1
Waukesha County .... No open season.
Quail, pheasants (Chinese, English, Mongolian), 8 years .... Oct. 1, 1915.
Partridge .... Oct. 1–Dec. 1.
Prairie chicken, grouse: In Adams, Ashland, Barron, Bayfield, Brown, Burnett, Buffalo, Chippewa, Clark, Crawford, Dodge, Douglas, Dunn, Eau Claire, Fond du Lac, Grant, Green Lake, Iowa, Jackson, Juneau, Lafayette, Marathon, Marinette, Marquette, Monroe, Oconto, Outagamie, Pepin, Pierce, Polk, Portage, Richland, Rusk, St. Croix, Sawyer, Shawano, Vernon, Washburn, Waupaca, Waushara, and Wood Counties .... Sept. 7–Oct. 2.
Prairie chicken, grouse: In rest of State .... Sept. 1, 1915.
Dove, swan .... No open season.
Woodcock, plover, snipe .... Sept. 7–Dec. 1.
Coot or mud hen, rail, rice hen, duck, goose, brant .... Sept. 7–Dec. 1.

Wyoming (1909–1913):

Deer (does and fawns, no open season) exceptions .... Oct. 1–Nov. 1.
Exceptions: Fremont, Lincoln, and Park Counties .... Sept. 1–Nov. 16.
Elk and male sheep in Lincoln, Park, and Fremont Counties north of Big Wind River and Bad Water Creek and also in Fremont County south of Sweetwater River .... Sept. 1–Nov. 16.
Elk and sheep in rest of State, moose, antelope, 5 years .... Sept. 1, 1918.
Quail (except in Crook County, Sept. 25, 1917), Mongolian pheasant .... Sept. 25, 1915.
Grouse (other than sage grouse), see exceptions .... Sept. 15–Nov. 16.
Exceptions: All grouse in Albany, Carbon, Laramie, and Sweetwater Counties .... July 15–Sept. 1.
Sage grouse (except in Sheridan County, Aug. 1, 1915) .... Aug. 1–Sept. 1.
Dove, swan .... No open season.
Black-breasted and golden plover, jacksnipe or Wilson snipe, yellowlegs .... Sept. 1–**Dec. 16.**
Curlew (Regulation No. 4) .... **Sept. 1, 1918.**
Rail, coot, gallinule .... **Sept. 1–Dec. 1.**
Duck, goose, **brant** .... Sept. 1–**Dec. 16.**

Alberta[1] (1906–1913):

Deer, moose, caribou .... Nov. 1–Dec. 15.
Antelope (male) .... Oct. 1.–Nov. 1.
Elk or wapiti .... Nov. 15, 1915.
Buffalo, female deer, moose, antelope, sheep, and young of all big game .... No open season.
Sheep (male), goat .... Sept. 1–Oct. 15.

---

[1] North of latitude 55° any game animal or bird, except elk and buffalo, may be killed at any time if needed for food.

	Open seasons.
Alberta—Continued.	
Partridge (except Hungarian partridge, no open season), grouse, prairie chicken, ptarmigan, pheasant (except English, no open season)	Oct. 1–Nov. 1.
Plover, curlew, sandpiper, snipe, shore bird, coot, rail, crane	Sept. 1–Jan. 1.
Duck,[1] swan	Aug. 23–Jan. 1.
British Columbia[2] (1898–1913):	
Deer, goat	Sept. 1–Dec. 15.
Bull moose, bull caribou, hare	Sept. 1–Jan. 1.[2]
Sheep, rams only	Sept. 1–Nov. 15.[2]
Buffalo, elk, and young of deer and females and young of moose, caribou, and sheep	No open season.
Bear	Sept. 1–July 15.
Quail, grouse, ptarmigan, English partridge, prairie chicken, pheasant, black game, capercailzie, snipe, duck, goose, swan	No open season.[2]
Plover, bittern, heron, meadowlark	Sept. 1–Mar. 1.
Manitoba (1909–1913):[3]	
Deer, elk or wapiti, moose, caribou or reindeer, antelope or cabri (males)	Dec. 1–Dec. 15.
Females and young of foregoing species and bison or buffalo	No open season.
Quail, woodcock, plover (except upland plover, July 1–Jan. 1), sandpiper, snipe	Aug. 1–Jan. 1.
Partridge, prairie chicken, grouse	Oct. 1–Oct. 20.
Dove	No open season.
Pheasant, 11 years	Oct. 1, 1920.
Duck	Sept. 1–Dec. 1.
New Brunswick (1909–1913):	
Deer, moose, caribou (cow and calf[4] moose and caribou, no open season)	Sept. 15–Dec. 1.
Partridge, woodcock, snipe	Sept. 15–Dec. 1.
Pheasant	No open season.
Teal, wood duck, dusky or black duck, goose, brant	Sept. 1–Dec. 2.
Shore or other birds on beaches, islands or lagoons bordering tidal waters of Northumberland Strait, Gulf of St. Lawrence, and Bay of Chaleur	Aug. 15–Jan. 1.
Newfoundland[5] (1902–1913):	
Elk, moose	No open season.
Caribou (except in a special region near Grand Lake, no open season)	Oct. 21–Feb. 1.[6]
Ptarmigan, willow grouse or partridge, plover, curlew, snipe, or "other wild or migratory birds (except wild geese)"	Sept. 20–Jan. 1.
Capercailzie, black game, 10 years	Oct. 12, 1917.
Nova Scotia (1908–1912):	
Deer, 3 years	Oct. 1, 1915.
Moose, bulls only (see exception)	Sept. 16–Nov. 16.
Exception: Cape Breton Island — Sept. 16, 1915	
Caribou (see exceptions)	Sept. 16, 1915.
Exceptions: Inverness and Victoria Counties, bulls only — Sept. 16–Oct. 16	
Hare, rabbit	Oct. 1–Mar. 1.
Quail, sharp-tailed grouse, ptarmigan, plover, curlew, yellow legs, sandpiper, teal, heron, bittern, beach birds, and waders	Aug. 15–Mar. 1.
Ruffed grouse or birch partridge	Oct. 1–Nov. 1.
Canada grouse (spruce partridge), chukar partridge, pheasant, capercailzie, black game	No open season.
Woodcock, Wilson snipe, blue-winged duck, wood duck	Sept. 1–Mar. 1.
Ontario[7] (1907–1913):	
Deer (except in Dufferin, Grey, Simcoe, and Wellington Counties, to Nov. 1, 1914; in Bruce County, Nov. 1, 1916; and except fawns, no open season)	Nov. 1–Nov. 16.[8]
Elk or wapiti	No open season.

[1] Except white-winged scoters, north of township 50, which may be taken at any time.

[2] The lieutenant governor in councilis empowered to open seasons each year for Columbian deer, quail, grouse, ptarmigan, English partridge, prairie chicken, pheasant, capercailzie, black game, snipe, duck, and goose. Orders in council have been made closing the season throughout the year on deer on the Queen Charlotte Islands; on white-tailed deer in the Similkameen and Okanogan districts; on moose south of latitude 52° except in the Columbia district of East Kootenay; and on mountain sheep in the Yale, Okanogan, and Similkameen districts.

[3] North of parallel 54° any game except pheasants may be taken at any time by settlers, farmers, surveyors, prospectors, explorers, or Indians in actual need of food, but not for sale or barter.

[4] Under 3 years of age and with horns bearing less than 3 tines 4 inches in length.

[5] Poor settlers may kill any birds, except capercailzie and black game, at any time, for immediate consumption by themselves or their families.

[6] Additional open season Aug. 1–Oct. 1.

[7] Lieutenant governor in council may alter close seasons in region north and west of French River, Lake Nipissing, and Mattawa River, and in the vicinity of Rondeau Park and close for a definite period seasons for any game animal or nonmigratory game bird whose numbers have diminished.

[8] Persons who put deer on their own lands, and their licensees, may hunt such deer Oct. 1–Nov. 16.

	Open seasons.
Ontario—Continued.	
Moose, caribou (bulls only)	Oct. 16–Nov. 16.[1]
Hare [2]	Oct. 1–Dec. 16.
Squirrel (black or gray) (except in Norfolk County, Nov. 15, 1915)	Nov. 15–Dec. 2.
Quail, wild turkey	Nov. 15–Dec. 2.
Partridge, grouse, prairie fowl, pheasant (see exceptions)	Oct. 15–Nov. 16.
Exceptions: Essex County, ruffed grouse, English ring neck pheasant, Hungarian partidge.... Oct. 15, 1914	
Lincoln and Welland Counties, English or Mongolian pheasant.... Oct. 15, 1914	
Capercailzie	Sept. 15, 1915.
Dove	No open season.[3]
Woodcock	Oct. 1–Nov. 16.
Plover, snipe, rail, other shore birds, duck and other waterfowl	Sept. 1–Dec. 16.[4]
Prince Edward Island (1906–1911):	
Hare, rabbit	Nov. 1–Feb. 1.
Partridge	Oct. 15–Nov. 15.
Plover, curlew	Aug. 1–Jan. 1.
Snipe, woodcock	Sept. 1–Jan. 1.
Yellow legs, shore and other birds along beaches or tidal marshes, duck	Aug. 20–Jan. 1.
Goose	Sept. 15–May 10.
Brant	Apr. 20–Jan. 1.
Quebec (1899–1913):	
Zone 1.[5] Deer, moose (see exceptions)	Sept. 1–Jan. 1.
Exceptions: In Labelle, Ottawa, Pontiac, and Temiscaming Counties. Oct. 1–Dec. 1	
Cow moose and young deer and moose	No open season.
Caribou (young, no open season)	Sept. 1–Feb. 1.
Hare	Oct. 15–Feb. 1.
Bear	Aug. 20–July 1.
Birch or swamp partridge	Sept. 1–Dec. 15.
White partridge or ptarmigan	Nov. 1–Feb. 1.
Woodcock, plover, curlew, tattler, sandpiper, snipe	Sept. 1–Feb. 1.
Widgeon, teal, duck (except sheldrake), gull, loon	Sept. 1–Mar. 1.[6]
Zone 2. Close seasons same as in Zone 1, except as follows:	
Caribou	Sept. 1.–Mar. 1.
Hare	Oct. 15–Mar. 1.
Birch or swamp partridge	Sept. 15–Feb. 1.
White partridge or ptarmigan	Nov. 15–Mar. 1.
Saskatchewan[7] (1905–1913):	
Deer, elk or wapiti, moose, caribou (males only)	Nov. 15–Dec. 1.[8]
Antelope (males only)	Oct. 1–Nov. 15.
Buffalo and females and young of above big game	No open season.
Partridge, pheasant, prairie chicken, grouse, ptarmigan	Sept. 15–Nov. 16.
English pheasant	No open season.
Plover, curlew, sandpiper, snipe, shore birds, coot, rail, duck, goose, swan, crane	Sept. 15–Jan. 1.
Northwest Territories[9] (1906):	
Deer, elk or wapiti, moose, caribou, goat, sheep	Dec. 1–Apr. 1.[10]
Musk ox	Oct. 15–Mar. 20.
Partridge, prairie chicken, grouse, pheasant	Sept. 1–Jan. 1.
Duck, goose, swan	Sept. 1–Jan. 15.
Yukon[11] (1902–1906):	
Deer, elk or wapiti, moose, caribou, sheep, goat, musk ox (males only)	Sept. 1–Mar. 1.
Bison or buffalo	No open season.
Partridge, prairie chicken, grouse, ptarmigan, pheasant	Sept. 1–Mar. 15.
Sandpiper, snipe, crane, duck, goose, swan	Aug. 10–June 1.

1 South of the Canadian Pacific R. R., between Mattawa and the Manitoba boundary, Nov. 1–16.

2 Cottontail rabbits (wood hares) may be killed during close season when damaging trees or shrubs.

3 Under act for protection of insectivorous birds, Rev. Stats., 1897, ch. 289, sec. 3.

4 Shore birds and waterfowl south of the Canadian Pacific, between Montreal and Toronto, and the Guelph and Goderich Railways, Sept. 15–Dec. 16.

5 Zone No. 1 comprises the whole Province, except that part of the counties of Chicoutimi and Saguenay east and north of the River Saguenay. Zone No. 2 comprises the excepted part of said counties.

6 Inhabitants of Zone 2 and Gaspé County may take these birds for food Aug. 1–June 1.

7 Lieutenant governor in council may extend close seasons over current year, within limits, on petition of six game guardians.

8 Applies north of line between Townships 34 and 35; south of said line, no open season.

9 Indians, inhabitants, travelers, explorers, and surveyors in need of food exempt. Governor in council may alter seasons.

10 Also July 15–Oct. 1.

11 Indians, explorers, surveyors, prospectors, miners, and travelers in need of food are exempt. Commissioner in council may alter seasons.

SHIPMENT OF GAME.

Shipment is the most important feature of the traffic in game. If permitted without limitation it is a great factor in game destruction. A realization of this fact has induced many of the States to prohibit export of all or certain kinds of game, and in a few instances all transportation even within the State. The subject may be conveniently considered under the following subheads: "Federal laws," and "State laws prohibiting export."

FEDERAL LAWS.

Federal laws affecting the shipment of game comprise the statutes regulating interstate commerce in game and the importation of birds from foreign countries, and those providing for the protection of birds and game on territory under immediate Federal jurisdiction.

They comprise: (1) Sections 241 to 244 of the Criminal Code (35 Stat., 1137), regulating the importation and interstate shipment of game;[1] (2) the tariff act, imposing duties on game, skins, and feathers imported from foreign countries; (3) the act regulating the introduction of eggs of game birds; (4) the game law of Alaska; and (5) provisions for protecting birds in the national parks,[2] national forests, and other Government reservations. These laws are more fully discussed in Bulletin No. 16 of the Biological Survey, entitled "Digest of Game Laws for 1901" (pp. 69–79). The full text of the new Alaskan game law of 1908, with the regulations now in force, is published in circulars of the Biological Survey. Sections 241, 242, 243, and 244 of the Criminal Code of the United States are as follows:

SEC. 241. The importation into the United States, or any Territory or District thereof, of the mongoose, the so-called "flying foxes" or fruit bats, the English sparrow, the starling, and such other birds and animals as the Secretary of Agriculture may from time to time declare to be injurious to the interests of agriculture or horticulture, is hereby prohibited; and all such birds and animals shall, upon arrival at any port of the United States, be destroyed or returned at the expense of the owner. No person shall import into the United States or into any Territory or District thereof, any foreign wild animal or bird, except under special permit from the Secretary of Agriculture: *Provided*, That nothing in this section shall restrict the importation of natural history specimens for museums or scientific collections, or of certain cage birds, such as domesticated canaries, parrots, or such other birds as the Secretary of Agriculture may designate. The Secretary of the Treasury is hereby authorized to make regulations for carrying into effect the provisions of this section.

SEC. 242. It shall be unlawful for any person to deliver to any common carrier for transportation, or for any common carrier to transport from any State, Territory, or District of the United States, to any other State, Territory, or District thereof, any foreign animals or birds, the importation of which is prohibited, or the dead bodies or parts thereof of any wild animals or birds, where such animals or birds have been

---

[1] These sections are sections 2, 3, and 4 of the Lacey Act as amended.

[2] The law governing the Yellowstone Park prohibits any person, or any stage, express, or railway company from receiving for transportation animals, birds, or fish taken in the park, under a penalty not exceeding $300. (28 Stat., ch. 72, sec. 4.)

killed or shipped in violation of the laws of the State, Territory, or District in which the same were killed, or from which they were shipped: *Provided*, That nothing herein shall prevent the transportation of any dead birds or animals killed during the season when the same may be lawfully captured, and the export of which is not prohibited by law in the State, Territory, or District in which the same are captured or killed: *Provided further*, That nothing herein shall prevent the importation, transportation, or sale of birds or bird plumage manufactured from the feathers of barnyard fowls.

SEC. 243. All packages containing the dead bodies, or the plumage, or parts thereof, of game animals, or game or other wild birds, when shipped in interstate or foreign commerce, shall be plainly and clearly marked, so that the name and address of the shipper, and the nature of the contents, may be readily ascertained on an inspection of the outside of such package.

SEC. 244. For each evasion or violation of any provision of the three sections last preceding, the shipper shall be fined not more than two hundred dollars; the consignee knowingly receiving such articles so shipped and transported in violation of said sections shall be fined not more than two hundred dollars; and the carrier knowingly carrying or transporting the same in violation of said sections shall be fined not more than two hundred dollars.

STATE LAWS PROHIBITING EXPORT.

Since the constitutionality of the Connecticut statute prohibiting export of certain game was established by the supreme court in 1896,[1] nonexport laws have been generally adopted, and at the present time every State prohibits the export of certain kinds of game. In most States sportsmen are allowed to carry a limited amount of game out of the State under special restrictions, and exceptions to the laws prohibiting export are also made in the case of birds and animals intended for propagation or reared in licensed preserves.

Restrictions on shipment from the State have now become so stringent that all the States west of the Mississippi River, prohibit export of all game protected by local laws. East of the Mississippi, laws prohibiting the export of all game, or, in some cases, all but one or two unimportant species, are in force in all the States except Kentucky and a small group along the coast from Massachusetts to North Carolina.

Special attention is called to the following table, which contains a list of the game prohibited from export by each State:

Export of game prohibited.

Alabama: All protected game.

Exceptions: Nonresident licensee may take with him or have carried to him, openly, game lawfully killed by him. State game and fish commissioner may issue $1 permit to any person to capture, kill, or export not more than 10 pairs of any one species of game or birds for scientific or propagating purposes.

Alaska: Deer, moose, caribou, sheep, goat, bear, or hides of these animals; wild birds, except eagles, or any parts thereof.

Exceptions: Specimens may be exported under restrictions imposed by the Secretary of Agriculture, and trophies of big game under licenses issued by the governor.[2]

Arizona: All protected game.

Exceptions: Deer or wild turkey may be exported under a $2 permit.

---

1 Geer v. Conn., 161 U. S., 519.

2 See p. 54 and also circulars of the Biological Survey, U. S. Department of Agriculture.

Arkansas: Deer (unless raised in captivity), wild turkey, wild fowl, game of any description except rabbits, which must be shipped open to view. (Squirrels can not be shipped out of Craighead, Dallas, Lafayette, and White Counties.) Local exceptions in Clay and Mississippi Counties.

California: All protected game.

Colorado: All protected game.

Exceptions: Game may be exported under permit from game commissioner if permit be attached and package plainly marked so as to show nature of contents. The following fees are charged for export permits: Elk, $10; deer, $5; sheep, $5; bird, 25 cents—in each case the edible portion alone.

Connecticut: Quail, ruffed grouse, woodcock.

Delaware: Rabbit, quail, partridge, woodcock. Squirrel, dove, rail, reedbird, goose, brant, for sale.

Exceptions: Holder of license may export 10 rabbits, 10 squirrels, 50 reedbirds, 50 rail, and 20 birds or fowl of any other species a week, lawfully killed by himself, under affidavit that the game is not for sale.

Florida: All protected game.

Exceptions: Nonresident licensee may carry out game as personal baggage; 10 pairs of any species of game birds may be exported for scientific or propagating purposes under $1 permit.

Georgia: All protected game from county or State.

Exception: Licensee may export game lawfully killed.

Idaho: All protected game.

Exceptions: Any hunter may export, under hunting license, big game lawfully taken, under a 50-cent permit obtained from a justice of the peace, probate judge, game warden, or deputy game warden on a sworn statement to issuing officer that game was not procured contrary to law. Mounted heads and stuffed birds legally secured may be exported.

Illinois: All protected game except dove, coot, rail taken in State.

Exceptions: Game may be exported under license from the State. Nonresident may take from State 50 birds killed by himself, if carried openly for inspection.

Indiana: Deer, quail, grouse, prairie chicken, pheasant, wild turkey, woodcock, duck, goose, brant, and other waterfowl.

Exception: Nonresident may take from State 15 birds killed by himself, if carried openly for inspection together with his license, or 45 if he has hunted for 3 or more days consecutively.

Iowa: All protected game.

Exception: Nonresident may take from State not more than 25 game birds or animals, if carried openly for inspection, and if hunting license be shown on request.

Kansas: All protected game.

Kentucky: Quail, partridge, grouse, pheasant, wild turkey killed in the State.

Louisiana: All protected game.

Exception: A nonresident licensee may carry with him out of the State, under his license, one day's bag limit of game, if not for sale. Game raised in private preserves and properly tagged may also be exported.

Maine: All protected game.

Exceptions: A resident of the State may export 1 deer in a season if open to view, tagged to show name and address of owner and accompanied by him, and under shipping license 1 moose, 5 partridges, 10 woodcock, and 10 ducks lawfully killed by himself. A nonresident may export under hunting license 1 moose and 2 deer lawfully killed by himself and may take home 10 partridges, 15 ducks, and 10 woodcock; he may also ship out one pair of game birds a month under a special 50-cent license. Live game may be exported for breeding, scientific, or advertising purposes, under permit of the commissioners of inland fisheries and game.

Maryland: *County provisions, as follows:*

Allegany—Deer, squirrel, rabbit, partridge or quail, pheasant, English pheasant, turkey, dove, woodcock from county (for sale).

Anne Arundel—All protected game, viz: Squirrel, rabbit, quail, partridge, pheasant, woodcock, snipe, plover, duck, goose, brant, swan from county.

Baltimore—Rabbit, squirrel, quail, partridge, pheasant, dove, woodcock from county.

Calvert—Rabbit, partridge, woodcock from county (for sale, barter, or trade).

Caroline—Rabbit, quail, partridge, woodcock from county.

Cecil—Squirrel, quail, grouse, woodcock, plover from county.

Dorchester—Squirrel, rabbit, quail, partridge, woodcock, dove (for sale).

Exception: Twelve quail or partridges, 6 squirrels, rabbits, woodcock, and doves may be taken out of the county at one time as personal baggage, if carried openly and not intended for sale.

Frederick—Squirrel, partridge, pheasant, woodcock from county (for sale).

Garrett—Rabbit, partridge, pheasant, wild turkey, woodcock from State.

Exception: Nonresident may take out game killed under his hunting license.

Kent—Squirrel, rabbit, and all birds from county (for sale, except under license).

Montgomery—Rabbit, partridge, quail, woodcock from county (for sale).

Queen Anne—Rabbit, partridge, woodcock from county (for sale).

Somerset—All game, viz: Squirrel, rabbit, quail or partridge, pheasant, dove, woodcock, duck, goose from county.

Washington—Deer, squirrel, rabbit, partridge, pheasant, dove, woodcock, turkey from county (for sale).

Wicomico—Quail or partridge from Wicomico and Worcester Counties considered as one territory.

Worcester—Rabbit, quail, woodcock from county.

Massachusetts: Quail, ruffed grouse, woodcock taken in State; other game illegally taken in State.

Exceptions: Nonresident may take 10 wild fowl or birds of all kinds out of the State under his hunting license. Quail reared in captivity under permit may be exported for propagation.

Michigan: All protected game.

Exceptions: (1) Deer may be transported outside the State to reach a point within the State.

(2) Nonresident licensee may take out, as hand baggage, 1 day's bag limit of birds, and may ship 1 deer under permit.

(3) Landowners and members of clubs owning game preserves may ship during open season under a $10 permit from State warden 20 ducks or other migratory birds killed by them on their own premises.

(4) Game reared in captivity and deer skins and green or mounted buck-deer heads may be exported under permit.

Minnesota: All protected game.

Exceptions: Nonresident licensee may ship home in open season under his license coupons 1 deer and 25 birds lawfully taken by himself. Domesticated big game may be exported under permit, and also deer and moose hides for tanning and moose heads for mounting.

Mississippi: All protected game.

Missouri: All protected game.

Exceptions: Game may be exported under resident or nonresident license if carried openly as baggage or express or in owner's possession and accompanied by him. Export for scientific or propagating purposes allowed under permit. Deer or elk raised in captivity may be shipped at any time.

Montana: All protected game.

Exception: Game lawfully killed may be exported in open season if accompanied by owner and resident's shipping permit from State game and fish warden or nonresident's hunting license; total shipment under one license not to exceed season's bag limit; packages to be labeled to show contents.

Nebraska: All protected game.

Exception: Nonresident may ship 50 birds out of State under hunting license, but must give common carrier invoice of number and kind of birds, must have details of shipment marked on license, and must accompany the shipment.

Nevada: All protected game.

New Hampshire:[1] Deer (except heads for mounting), elk, moose, caribou, quail, partridge, ruffed grouse, pheasant, woodcock, Wilson snipe, dove, plover, yellowlegs, sandpiper, rail, duck (except sheldrake), and all "beach" birds.

Exceptions: Deer may be exported by resident if accompanied to office of carrier by owner, shipped open to view, properly tagged, and labeled with name of actual owner. Nonresident may export, under his hunting license, 2 deer and 12 birds, carried open to view, on notice of number and kind to the commissioner who issued the license.

New Jersey: Hare, rabbit, squirrel, and all protected game birds.

Exceptions: Nonresident licensee may carry openly from the State 10 rabbits, 50 reed birds, 50 rail, and 15 other game birds a day. Live deer may be exported for propagation on payment of additional fee of $5 for each animal; English, ringneck or other pheasants, mallard and black ducks, and deer raised in inclosed preserves may be exported for sale if properly tagged.

New Mexico: Export for market of all game taken in the State, except plover, curlew, snipe, mallard and black duck.

Exception: The State warden is authorized to issue transportation permits at $1 each ($2 in case of deer), and also to permit export of game or birds for scientific or propagating purposes.

New York: Game or birds taken in the State.

Exceptions: Nonresident may export one deer and one day's bag limit of other game under permit. Foreign game or game raised in licensed preserves may be exported unaccompanied by the owner in any quantity when duly marked and tagged. Game for propagation and heads and skins of quadrupeds and game birds legally captured may be exported.

North Carolina:[2] Quail, partridge, pheasant, grouse, wild turkey, snipe, shore or beach bird, woodcock taken in State.

Exception: Nonresident may take out of State under his hunting license 50 quail (partridges), 12 grouse, 2 turkeys, and 50 beach birds or snipe in a season. Export permitted under permit of Audubon Society of ruffed grouse, wild turkey, woodcock, snipe, and other shore birds, for propagation.

---

1 Blue Mountain Forest Association permitted to ship deer, elk, and moose killed in its preserve.

2 Export is also prohibited by the following local laws: *Deer*, Cherokee, Craven, Hyde (Currituck Township); *squirrel*, Craven; *quail*, Alexander (for sale—except 50 at one time by nonresident licensee), Catawba, Cherokee, Clay, Cleveland (3 years), Craven, Harnett, Henderson, Iredell, Jackson, Montgomery, Rutherford, Stanly (for sale—except by owner or lessee of land on which killed), Surry (for sale), Swain (live), Union (for sale), Yadkin (for sale); *wildfowl*, Craven (from State), Brunswick (Mar. 10–Nov. 10), Dare (Mar. 10–Nov. 10), New Hanover (Mar. 10–Nov. 10), Stanly (for sale—except by owner or lessee of land on which killed); *other game birds*, Cherokee (pheasant, dove, woodcock, robin, snipe), Craven (wild turkey, dove, woodcock), Montgomery (pheasant, wild turkey, dove), Stanly (all game birds), Tyrrell (woodcock, snipe—unless killed Nov. 1–Feb. 1), Union (dove, lark—for sale).

North Dakota: All protected game, except golden plover and woodcock.

Exceptions: Nonresident licensee may carry with him from State prairie chickens and doves, not exceeding 20 in all, and plover, snipe, ducks, and geese, not exceeding 50 in all, open to view, labeled with his name and address and number of his license. Domesticated game may be exported under written permission of board of control.

Ohio: Squirrel, quail, ruffed grouse or pheasant, introduced pheasant, dove, woodcock, plover, snipe, shore birds, rail, coot (mud hen), duck, goose, swan taken in the State.

Exception: Nonresident may take with him from State under his hunting license 25 pieces of game.

Oklahoma: All protected game.

Exception: Nonresident licensee may carry to his home two days' bag limit of game birds.

Oregon: All protected game.

Exceptions: Game birds raised in captivity for breeding purposes and pinioned may be shipped under tag. Game for propagation or scientific purposes may be exported under permit.

Pennsylvania: All protected game taken in the State.

Exceptions: Nonresident licensee may take with him from the State one day's bag labeled with his name and address and number of his license. Elk raised in captivity may be exported under regulations of commission. Live English, Mongolian, and Chinese pheasants raised in captivity may be exported.

Rhode Island: Quail, ruffed grouse, woodcock, plover, curlew, yellowlegs, snipe, sandpiper, shore, marsh and beach birds.

Exception: Nonresident may take with him from the State under his hunting license, open to view, 10 wildfowl or birds the export of which is otherwise prohibited by law.

South Carolina: All game birds or animals taken in the State.

Exception: Licensee may carry openly 2 deer, 50 partridges, 12 ruffed grouse, 4 wild turkeys, 50 beach birds, 50 ducks and geese in a season.

South Dakota: All protected game.

Exceptions: Two deer. A certificate—good for five days—that such game was lawfully killed must be obtained from a justice of the peace and given to the carrier. Any resident or nonresident may carry out of the State any game bird legally in possession. Game or game birds raised in captivity may be exported under written permission of State game warden.

Tennessee: All protected game.

Exception: Nonresident may take with him from the State 50 ducks or 30 pieces of other game, but must present to some officer or employee of common carrier his hunting license and sworn statement that his game will not be sold.

Texas: All wild animals, wild birds, and wild fowl found in the State.

Exception: Nonresident licensee may take with him from the State 3 male deer, 75 ducks (if killed in three consecutive days by himself), and one day's bag limit of other birds, under affidavit that his game will not be sold.

Utah: All protected game.

Exception: Nonresident licensee may take one day's bag out of State under permit.

Vermont: Deer, gray squirrel, quail, ruffed grouse or partridge, plover, English snipe, woodcock, duck, goose.

Exceptions: Nonresident licensee may export 1 deer and one day's bag of game birds under license, but must accompany shipment. Resident may export, open to view, the season limit of game or game birds under his license by having the license marked with shipping point, destination, and number of each kind of game. Also game raised in private preserves may be exported when duly marked and tagged.

Virginia: All protected game except waterfowl legally killed.

Exceptions: During open season nonresident may, under his hunting license, take with him out of the State, or as baggage on the same conveyance, 1 deer, 50 quail or partridges, 10 pheasants or grouse, 3 wild turkeys, and 25 of each, or 100 in all, of plover, snipe, sandpipers, willets, tatlers, and curlew, if killed or captured by himself and shipped open to view and plainly labeled with his name and address. Any citizen of State may ship from the State, as a gift and not for sale (which fact must be stated on shipping tag), 1 deer, 18 quail or partridges, 6 pheasants, 3 wild turkeys, and if open to view and plainly labeled with names and addresses of donor and donee, and number of each kind of bird so shipped.

Washington: All protected game.

Exceptions: Nonresident may export one season's limit of big game and one day's bag limit of birds under his hunting license, if accompanied by affidavit that the game was killed by him and is not for sale. Export of game animals and birds raised in captivity permitted.

West Virginia: All protected game.

Wisconsin: All protected game, except rabbit, squirrel, and coot (mud hen).

Exceptions: During open season nonresident may take out of State under his hunting license, in personal possession or as baggage or express, accompanying same to State line, 1 deer and not more than 30 game animals and birds of all kinds, provided packages are plainly marked so as to show the names and addresses of shipper and consignee and number of each kind of game, and, in case of deer, have proper coupons attached. Park boards allowed to ship, under permit of State game warden, live animals and game birds for park purposes. Shipment allowed of domesticated deer, moose, elk, and caribou and game birds properly tagged, under permit of State game warden.

Wyoming: All protected game.

Exceptions: Smithsonian Institution or other well-known scientific institutions may export any game animals or birds under permit of State game commission.

Export of 1 hide, 1 scalp, 1 head, 1 pair of tusks, 1 skin, 1 mounted head, 1 mounted specimen, of any big game except moose permitted upon affidavit that they were taken from animals lawfully killed, the payment of 25 cents to the justice of the peace of precinct where affiant lives, and attachment of the tag issued by him; a nonresident (or resident, when necessary to cross territory of another State to reach his home) may export under his hunting license 20 dead game birds and the carcass, head, antlers, scalp, skin, and teeth of any animal lawfully killed; exchange of game animals and birds for others for liberation in Wyoming allowed under permit of the State game commission; big game, except moose, captured and held for propagation may be exported after five years.

Alberta: All protected game.

Exceptions: Minister of agriculture on receipt of a $5 fee may grant a permit to export for propagation or scientific purposes one pair of each species of big game and game birds. The lieutenant governor in council may grant permits for a greater number. The minister of agriculture may also issue permits for export of game for other purposes at the rate of $5 for each head of big game and $1 per dozen for game birds. The holder of a general nonresident license may take with him out of the Province as trophies, heads, skins, and hoofs of big game legally killed by him. Any person may export mounted or branded heads at a fee of $1 for each head.

British Columbia: All protected game, except bears.

Exceptions: Heads, horns, and skins of big game lawfully killed by the shipper may be shipped under his hunting license and written permission of minister charged with enforcement of act. Any animal or bird, dead or alive, may be exported for scientific, zoological, or Government purposes under permit of provincial secretary. Live game birds or animals held in captivity under written permission of provincial game warden may be exported.

Manitoba: All protected game.

Exceptions: Minister of agriculture and immigration may direct chief game guardian to export not more than 12 animals or birds for propagation and may issue permit to export heads and skins of big game animals, and any game birds, except grouse, prairie chicken, and partridge, but not more than 100 geese and swans or 50 ducks, and these only under nonresident license. (No export of ducks permitted before October 1.) The following export fees are charged: Deer or deer head, $2 each; head of elk, moose, or caribou, or carcass, $5 each; any hide, 10 cents. No export fee required of nonresident licensee.

New Brunswick:[1] All protected game.

Exception: Surveyor general may issue special license to export game alive or dead.

Newfoundland: Caribou (antlers, heads, or skins), or partridge, willow or other grouse for sale.

Exceptions: Minister of marine and fisheries may issue licenses to export caribou for breeding or scientific purposes. Nonresident may export 3 stag caribou under hunting license and export permit (fee, 50 cents); resident may export antlers, head, or skin of caribou under export permit; but not, in either case, for sale.

Nova Scotia: All protected game.

Exceptions: Holder of general license may ship out of Province 1 moose lawfully shot by himself. Mounted heads and dressed skins and live mammals or birds for propagation or scientific purposes may be exported under permit from provincial secretary.

Ontario: All wild game animals and birds.

Exceptions: One deer, 1 bull moose, 1 bull caribou, and 100 ducks may be exported under nonresident hunting license if shipping coupon and, if required, affidavit of lawful killing be attached and contents of packages be open to view. Lawfully imported game and deer, moose, elk, or caribou held by private ownership may be exported.

Prince Edward Island: All game except geese and brant.

Exception: Nonresident licensee may carry out of Province 12 birds killed by himself.

Quebec: Native deer, moose, caribou, or parts thereof, except under permit from Minister of colonization, mines, and fisheries (fee not to exceed $5), or under tags attached to nonresident licenses, and not later than 15 days after close of season.

Saskatchewan: All protected game.

Exceptions: Minister of agriculture may grant permits to export for propagation for public parks and zoological gardens or scientific purposes 1 pair of each species of big game and game birds upon payment of $5, or a specified number on application of another Province or State. Minister may issue permits to export big game (fee $5 per head), ducks, or geese (fee $1 per dozen, limit 5 dozen per season.)

Yukon: Protected game can be exported by a nonresident only under a hunting license and a shipping permit issued by the commissioner of the Territory, or a game guardian. Permits export of one head of each of the following kinds of big game: Moose, caribou, sheep, and goat.

Canada also has a general law prohibiting export of deer (except those raised on private preserves), wild turkeys, quail, partridges, prairie fowl, and woodcock, but permitting each nonresident to ex-

---

[1] Except in the case of partridge the prohibition applies only to common carriers.

port two deer[1] in a year at certain ports within 15 days after the close of the open season, under permit of the collector of customs of the port from which export is made. The ports of export are: Halifax and Yarmouth, Nova Scotia; Macadam Junction, New Brunswick; Quebec and Montreal, Quebec; Ottawa, Kingston, Niagara Falls, Fort Erie, Windsor, Sault Ste. Marie, and Port Arthur, Ontario; and such others as the minister of customs may designate.

Those who visit Canada to hunt, camp, etc., must deposit with the customs officer at the port of entry an amount equal to the duty (30 per cent of appraised value) on their guns, canoes, tents, cooking utensils, and kodaks. If these articles are taken out within six months at the same port, the deposit will be returned. But members of shooting or fishing clubs that own preserves in Canada and have filed a guaranty with the Canadian commissioner of customs may present club membership certificates in lieu of making the deposit. They must, however, pay duty on all ammunition and provisions.

SALE.

Legislation restricting the sale of game is passing through a transition stage. Some States prohibit the sale of game throughout the year, others only in close season, and between these extremes may be found all gradations and exceptions, such as restrictions prohibiting sale of game outside the State or for export, and exemptions allowing sale for a few days in the close season. The difficulty of tabulating such regulations is increased by the fact that in addition to the special sale laws, close seasons and provisions regarding possession must be taken into consideration. In consulting the following summary, therefore, it will be necessary to bear in mind three different classes of restrictions: "Sale in close season," "Sale in open season," and "Sale prohibited all the year."

SALE IN CLOSE SEASON.

In general, the sale of game is prohibited during the close season but a brief additional open period is sometimes provided in order to permit dealers to close out stock on hand at the end of the hunting season. In Louisiana an extension of three days is allowed. In Colorado, Illinois, Tennessee, and British Columbia the sale season includes the open season and the following five days for all or certain kinds of game. An extension of 10 days for sale is added to the open season in New Brunswick; 15 days in Alaska, New Jersey, and Quebec; 30 days in Pennsylvania; 60 days in Yukon; 3 months (for geese and brant) in New Brunswick; and until the following 1st of January in Ontario.

[1] Except from Ontario (see above).

SALE IN OPEN SEASON.

In order to counteract a tendency on the part of market hunters to anticipate the opening of the season, the sale of certain game is sometimes prohibited at the beginning of the open season, as during the first two days in Illinois, the first three in Nova Scotia and Quebec, and the first month in British Columbia.

SALE PROHIBITED ALL THE YEAR.

Forty-seven States[1] and most of the Provinces of Canada now prohibit sale of all or certain kinds of game at all seasons. In Alabama, Arizona, Arkansas, Colorado, Florida, Georgia, Idaho, Iowa, Kansas, Mississippi, Missouri, Montana, Nebraska, Nevada, Oklahoma, Oregon, South Carolina, Texas, Washington, West Virginia, and Wyoming, the sale, and in Delaware the resale, of all protected game is prohibited; in Michigan and Ohio, of all game except rabbits; in New York and New Jersey of all game except rabbits and that raised in licensed preserves and a few imported species; in Minnesota, of all game except that raised in captivity; in Wisconsin, of all game except rabbits, squirrels, coots, and rails; in California, of all game except ducks; in Utah and Manitoba, of all big game and upland game. In a few instances prohibitions against the sale of certain game are so general as to afford protection over a considerable area in adjoining States. Thus, ruffed grouse can not be sold in any State or Province along the Canadian border except Quebec. Practically every State in which prairie chickens occur now prohibits their sale or export.

The following statement shows the kinds of game the sale of which is prohibited throughout the year. The sale of all other game is so generally prohibited during the close season as to render a detailed enumeration unnecessary, but when an extension of a few days is added to the open season or a special season is provided for either possession or sale, attention is called to this exemption under the heading "Permitted."

Sale of game prohibited throughout the year.

Alabama: All protected game.

Alaska: Heads, hides, and skins of all protected game. Deer until August 15, 1914.

Permitted: Carcasses of all game may be sold during the open season and 15 days thereafter.

Arizona: All protected game.

Arkansas: All "game, wild fowl, or birds whatsoever," except deer raised in captivity, bears, rabbits, opossums, raccoons, and squirrels.[2]

[1] Omitting Alaska, which prohibits sale only of heads, skins, and trophies and deer in southeastern Alaska until Aug. 15, 1914; District of Columbia, which prohibits sale only in close season; North Carolina, which prohibits sale in only a few counties.

[2] Squirrels killed in Ouachita and Union Counties can not be sold, and no squirrels can be sold in Craighead, Dallas, and Lafayette Counties. Wildfowl may be sold in the Chickasawba district in Mississippi County.

California: Deer meat and hides of female deer, or those from which evidence of sex has been removed, all other protected game, except cottontail rabbit, duck, and black brant.

Permitted: Game may be sold under license. Pheasants reared in captivity or imported from foreign country may be sold at any time under permit.

Colorado: All game taken in the State.

Permitted: Domestic game may be sold by hotels, restaurants, etc., during the open season and five days thereafter, or during the limits of a storage permit. Imported game (under license) and game taken from licensed private parks and lakes may be sold at any time if accompanied by an invoice.

Connecticut: Quail, ruffed grouse, Hungarian partridge, woodcock.

Delaware: All protected game, except that a resident lawfully taking game may sell plover, snipe, and ducks anywhere and other game in his own county; restaurants buying from such persons may serve game in open season.

Florida: All protected game.

Georgia: All protected game, except migratory ducks.

Idaho: All protected game.

Illinois: All protected game, except dove, coot, rail.

Permitted: Deer bred in captivity may be sold October 1 to February 1; cock pheasants may be sold by breeders (under permit) November 1 to February 1; doves may be sold from the third day of the open season to the fifth day of the close season; and legally killed game imported from other States from October 1 to February 1.

Indiana: Quail.

Iowa: All protected game.

Kansas: All protected game.

Permitted: Game reared in captivity may be sold under permit.

Kentucky: Quail, partridge, grouse, pheasant, wild turkey, killed in the State.

Louisiana: All protected game, except snipe, rail coots, poule d'eau, ducks, geese, and brant, which may be sold during open season and three days thereafter, but not later than March 1.

Permitted: Game reared in captivity may be sold during the open season.

Maine: Deer or moose for export. All protected game birds for any purpose.

Permitted: Deer may be sold by local dealers under license.

Maryland:

Allegany—Deer, quail, grouse, English pheasant, wild turkey, dove, woodcock.

Anne Arundel—All game except squirrel, rabbit, and raccoon.

Baltimore—Rabbit, squirrel, quail, ruffed grouse, dove, pheasant, woodcock, for export.

Calvert—Rabbit, quail, woodcock, for export for sale.

Cecil—Squirrel, quail, grouse, woodcock, plover.

Dorchester—Rabbit, squirrel, quail, partridge, dove, woodcock, wood duck, for export.

Frederick—Squirrel, partridge, pheasant, woodcock, taken in county.

Garrett—Rabbit, partridge, quail, pheasant, wild turkey, woodcock, for export.

Montgomery—Rabbit, quail, partridge, woodcock, for export.

Somerset—Rabbit, quail or partridge, woodcock, dead or alive, for any other purpose than as food within the county or for propagation; or any game for export.

Washington—Deer, squirrel, rabbit, partridge, pheasant, wild turkey, dove, woodcock.

Wicomico—Quail or partridge for export (from Wicomico and Worcester Counties considered as one territory).

Worcester—Rabbit, quail, woodcock (except to consumer).

Permitted: Baltimore City—Ruffed grouse may be sold October 1–December 25.

Massachusetts: Deer and quail taken in the State, gray squirrel, ruffed grouse, prairie chicken, sharp-tailed grouse, pheasant, Hungarian partridge, woodcock, piping plover, and killdeer plover.

Permitted: Dealers or persons in the cold-storage business may sell imported quail lawfully obtained during November and December, and may sell at any time hares or rabbits lawfully secured. Live quail for propagation may be sold under permit. Quail and Hungarian partridges raised in captivity under written permit may be sold for propagation. Deer and pheasants raised in captivity may be sold for any purpose.

Michigan: All protected game, except rabbits.

Permitted: Game raised in captivity may be sold alive within State and, under $1 permit, alive or dead without the State.

Minnesota: All protected game.

Permitted: Game animals (under permit) and birds (under tag) raised in captivity may be sold at any time.

Mississippi: All protected game.

Missouri: All protected game.

Permitted: Deer or elk reared in captivity may be sold under regulations of commissioner.

Montana: All protected game.

Permitted: Merchant, hotel, or restaurant keeper may sell game not killed in the State.

Nebraska: All protected game.

Nevada: All protected game.

New Hampshire: Deer (except 2), gray squirrel (to Oct. 1, 1919), ruffed grouse or partridge, woodcock.

New Jersey: Deer, squirrel, or game birds except waterfowl, or any game belonging to a family, any species of which is native to and protected by the State.

Permitted: Rabbits and waterfowl; certain imported game; and also deer, pheasants, black and mallard ducks raised in preserves or coming from another State may be sold at all times of the year if properly tagged.

New Mexico: All protected game taken in the State except plover, curlew, and snipe.

Permitted: Sale of game raised in licensed preserves.

New York: All game belonging to a family any species or subspecies of which is native to and protected by the State.

Permitted: Varying hares and rabbits during open season, and unplucked carcasses of pheasants, Scotch grouse, European black game, European black plover, red-legged partridge, and Egyptian quail, and carcasses of European red deer, fallow deer, roebuck, and reindeer imported from without the United States may be sold under license at any time.

American elk, white-tailed deer, European red deer, fallow deer, roebuck, pheasants, mallard, and black ducks raised in captivity under license, may be killed and sold under license at any time; breeder of pheasants may, under license, kill by shooting his surplus cock pheasants during February.

North Carolina: Local restrictions in Alexander, Brunswick, Cabarrus, Cherokee, Cleveland, Craven, Harnett, Henderson, Iredell, Mecklenburg, Moore, New Hanover, Fender, Randolph, Richmond, Rutherford, Scotland, Stanly, Transylvania, and Union Counties.

North Dakota: All protected game, except woodcock and plover.

Permitted: Hides of big game lawfully taken may be sold at any time. Domesticated game may be sold on written permission of the game board of control.

Ohio: All protected game, except rabbits.

Oklahoma: All protected game.

Permitted: Domesticated game animals and birds, and heads, hides, and horns of big game lawfully killed may be sold.

Oregon: All protected game.

Permitted: Game birds and animals imported from without the United States may be sold Sept. 1–Mar. 1, and game or animals raised in captivity under permit at any time, upon being properly tagged by commissioner or deputy.

Pennsylvania: Wild deer or elk taken in State; quail, ruffed grouse (pheasant), wild turkey, and woodcock (wherever taken).

Permitted: Squirrel, rabbit or hare, bear, reedbird, black-breasted and golden plover, Wilson or jacksnipe, yellow legs, coot or mud hen, rail, taken in State, may be sold during open season and 30 days thereafter; waterfowl may be sold Sept. 1–Jan. 1. Game or birds used for propagating purposes may be sold at any time under authority of game commissioners.

Rhode Island: Quail, ruffed grouse, pheasant, woodcock, plover, yellow legs, snipe, curlew, sandpiper, shore, marsh, and beach birds.

South Carolina: All protected game.

South Dakota: All protected game, except dove, golden and upland plover, and woodcock.

Permitted: Hides, heads, or horns of big game lawfully killed may be sold at any time. Game or game birds raised in captivity may be sold under written permission of State game warden.

Tennessee: Quail, robin. In Dyer County also wild turkey.

Permitted: All game except quail and robin may be sold in the State during the open season and five days thereafter.

Texas: All game animals, hides and horns, wild birds, and wild fowl found in the State.

Utah: Deer, elk, antelope, sheep, quail, partridge, grouse, prairie chicken, sage hen, pheasant, Mongolian. Chinese, and English pheasant, dove.

Permitted: 25 in all of shore birds and waterfowl may be sold in a day to private parties.

Vermont: All protected game birds or species belonging to any family native to the State.

Permitted: Deer may be sold during the open season and for a "reasonable time thereafter," and hares and rabbits during the open season. Game from private preserves may be sold under tag in accordance with regulations of the commissioner.

Virginia: Quail or partridge, grouse or pheasant, robin, woodcock.

Clarke County.—Rabbit, squirrel, wild turkey (outside of county).

Frederick, Shenandoah Counties.—Wild turkey (by nonresidents of Virginia).

Washington: All protected game.

Permitted: Hides and horns of big game legally killed, and propagated game animals and birds may be sold for propagation purposes at any time.

West Virginia: All protected game, except reedbird and rail.

Wisconsin: All protected game, except rabbit, squirrel, coot (mud hen), and rail.

Permitted: Domesticated deer, moose, elk, caribou, and game birds may be sold under permit of State fish and game warden.

Wyoming: All protected game.

Permitted: Sale of 1 live game animal, 1 skin, 1 mounted head, 1 mounted specimen, 1 pair of tusks, 1 hide, 1 scalp, and 1 head of any big game, except moose, on affidavit that they were lawfully captured or were taken from animals lawfully killed and payment of 25-cent fee to the justice of the peace of precinct where affiant lives and attachment of tag issued by him. Sale of the natural increase of any big game, except moose, captured and held for propagation.

Alberta: Grouse, partridge, pheasant, prairie chicken, ptarmigan; other game birds Mar. 1-Sept. 20.

Permitted: The flesh of big game and game birds may be sold under $10 license. Heads of big game before being sold must be stamped by minister of agriculture at fees of $5 for elk, caribou, moose, and sheep, and $2 for deer, antelope, and goat.

British Columbia: Elk, quail, grouse, ptarmigan, prairie chicken, English partridge, pheasant, swan, female and young of deer, moose, caribou, or sheep, heads of moose, caribou, and sheep.

Permitted: Male deer may be sold September 1-November 16; male moose, caribou, sheep, goats, and hares after October 1; snipe, ducks, and geese, October 1-December 1; and plover during the open season and five days thereafter. Lieutenant governor in council may alter or extend sale seasons.

Manitoba: Deer, elk, moose, caribou, antelope (except heads and hides), quail, grouse, pheasant, partridge, prairie chicken, woodcock, plover, snipe, sandpiper. Ducks can not be sold before October 1.

Permitted: Possession of grouse, prairie chickens, and partridges allowed for forty-five days, and ducks for three months, after close of hunting season. Deer for private use may be possessed at any time on proof of legal killing.

New Brunswick: Partridge until September 15, 1915.

Permitted: Geese and brant during open season and until March 1, and other game during open season and (under license) ten days thereafter. Keepers of hotels, inns, boarding houses, or restaurants may serve game during open season and fifteen days thereafter. Surveyor general may issue $1 licenses to dealers permitting sale by each of 3 deer and heads of same to taxidermists, and licenses to deal in hides or skins of game animals with fees of $25 to nonresidents or aliens and $2 to residents.

Newfoundland: Capercailzie, black game.

Permitted: Caribou may be sold from August 1 to January 1.

Nova Scotia: Deer to 1915, caribou, pheasant, blackcock, capercailzie, Canada grouse (spruce partridge), chukar partridge.

Permitted: Moose may be sold from September 17 to December 1. Rabbit, December 1 to March 1. Any game bird other than those above mentioned during the open season with the exception of the first three days.

Ontario: Quail, partridge, woodcock, snipe, to September 15, 1914.

Permitted: All other native game may be sold during the open season[1] by the person killing it and by dealers during open season and until the following January 1 under license. Imported game may be sold under special regulations and licenses.

Quebec:[2]

Permitted: All game lawfully taken may be sold from the third day of the open season to the fifteenth day of the close season. Hotels, restaurants, and clubs may serve, under license, all game lawfully taken, except birch or swamp partridge. Live animals, and skins and heads of animals lawfully taken may be sold.

Saskatchewan: Sheep, goat, or prairie chicken, grouse, pheasant, ptarmigan, or other member of the Gallinæ.

Yukon:

Permitted: Deer, elk, moose, caribou, bison, musk oxen, sheep, and goats may be sold during the open season and sixty days thereafter.

LIMITS.

Laws limiting the amount of game which can be killed in a day or a season are now in force throughout the United States, except in Kentucky, Rhode Island, Virginia, and the District of Columbia, and in all the Canadian Provinces, except Prince Edward Island. These measures are of comparatively recent origin. One of the first statutes of the kind was that passed in Iowa in 1878 (ch. 156, sec. 3) limiting the killing or possession of prairie chickens, snipe, woodcock, quail, and ruffed grouse to 25 in a day.[3] Maine, in 1883 (ch. 185, sec. 1), limited the number of big game which an individual might kill in a season to 1 moose, 2 caribou, and 3 deer, and New York, in 1886 (ch. 194, sec. 1), likewise limited the number of deer to 3. In spite of the objection often urged against such statutes—that they are impossible of enforcement and easily evaded—experience has shown them to

[1] Seasons depend on regulations of game commission.

[2] Lieutenant governor in council may prohibit sale of any game for three years or less or prolong any existing period of prohibition for three years or less.

[3] This statute was, however, preceded by one enacted in 1874 limiting the shipment of game birds to a dozen a day, provided the birds were not shipped for sale (ch. 69, sec. 1).

constitute one of the most effective features of modern game legislation. They have been tested in the courts and upheld by the supreme courts of several States, notably those of Maine and Wisconsin.[1]

When restrictions on limits are extended to possession and shipment as well as killing, and the total amount of game allowed a party made less than the quantity allowed the individual members of the party, little difficulty is experienced in enforcing the statute. Moreover, among law-abiding sportsmen the incentive to make large bags is removed when the act is declared illegal.

In recent years bag limits have been materially reduced, and only a few States now allow more than 2 deer a season or 1 head of other big game, while the usual limits per day in the case of birds are 10 grouse or woodcock, 15 quail, and 25 waterfowl. In Canada, where the country is not so closely settled, bag limits on most game are fewer and more liberal than in the United States.

Limits fixed by law for the capture of game.

Alabama: One deer, 2 turkey gobblers, 25 of each other kind of birds a day.

Alaska: Six deer, 2 moose, 3 caribou, 3 sheep, and 3 brown bears a season; 25 grouse, ptarmigan, shore birds or waterfowl a day.

Arizona: Two deer, 3 turkeys a season, 25 each of quail or ducks, 35 doves or white wings a day.

Arkansas: No limits, except in the following counties: Deer, Bradley 3, Dallas 3, Desha 4, Phillips 4 (or 1 for each member of party), Chicot 5, a season; quail, Bradley and Dallas 300 a season or 25 a day for each member of party. Monroe, 3 deer, 2 bears, 100 quail, 5 wild turkeys, and 100 ducks a season; party limits, 1 deer, 1 bear, 10 quail, 1 wild turkey, 15 ducks for each member.

California: Two deer, 12 tree squirrels a season; 15 cotton-tail or bush rabbits, 4 grouse, 4 sage hens, 10 mountain quail, 20 each of desert or valley quail, doves, plover, curlew, snipe, or other shore birds, and ibises, and 25 ducks and black sea brant a day; 50 ducks or black-sea brant per week.

Colorado: Twenty game birds a day, 30 in possession at one time. Persons under 12 years of age limited to half this number of birds.

Connecticut: Five each of quail and ruffed grouse a day, 36 a year; 35 rail, 50 each of plover, snipe, shore birds a day.

Delaware: Six animals, 50 rail, 20 ducks, 12 other birds or fowl, except plover, snipe and reedbirds, a day.

District of Columbia: No limits.

Florida: Three deer, 5 turkeys, and 500 other game birds a year; 1 deer, 2 turkeys, 20 quail, and 25 each of other species a day.

Georgia: Three deer, 3 turkeys a season; 40 doves or snipe, and 25 each of any other species of game birds a day.

Idaho: Two deer, 1 elk, 1 ibex, 1 goat, 1 sheep a season; 18 quail, 12 each of partridges, sage hens, grouse pheasants, 24 doves, plover, snipe, ducks, 4 geese, 1 swan a day; but not more than 24 of all kinds in possession at one time.

Illinois: Fifteen squirrels, 12 quail, 3 prairie chickens, 15 doves, 15 shore birds, 15 coots, 15 rail, 15 ducks, 10 geese, 10 brant, 15 other waterfowl a day.

Indiana: Fifteen quail, 15 ducks or other waterfowl a day; 45 birds in possession as result of 3 or more days' consecutive hunting.

Iowa: Twenty-five each of all animals, birds, and game a day; 50 ducks in possession at one time.

Kansas: Twenty each of dove, plover, duck, 12 snipe and 6 each of geese and brant a day.

Kentucky: No limits.

Louisiana: Two deer a day or in possession at one time, 5 a season; 10 squirrels, 1 turkey gobbler, 25 doves, ducks, poule d'eau, or chorooks, 50 snipe, 15 of any other game birds a day. Market hunters, 50 ducks or poule d'eau a day.

Maine: One moose, 2 deer a season (except in Androscoggin, Cumberland, Knox, Kennebec, Lincoln, Sagadahoc, Waldo, and York Counties, limit 1, and in lumber camps, limit 6); 5 each of ruffed grouse and plover, and 10 each of woodcock, snipe, and ducks, and 50 sandpipers a day.

Maryland: One deer a season; 12 rabbits, 12 squirrels, 15 quail (partridges), 6 ruffed grouse (pheasants), 3 English pheasants, 2 wild turkeys, 25 doves, 12 woodcock, 12 jacksnipe a day; 50 rail (ortolan) per tide.

Exceptions.—Baltimore, per day: 6 rabbits, 1 jack rabbit, 8 squirrels, 10 quail (partridges), 2 ruffed grouse (pheasants), 1 English pheasant, 1 ring-neck pheasant, 1 wild turkey, 10 doves, 8 woodcock, 12 jack snipe; per tide: 28 rail. Calvert, per day: 6 rabbits, 12 partridges. Cecil, per day: 5 rabbits, 6 squirrels, 12 quail (partridges), 4 ruffed grouse (pheasants), 12 woodcock, 15 snipe, 50 rail, 50 blackbirds, 20 Bartramian sandpipers (grass plover), 20 marsh plover, and 25 each of teal, wood, mallard, black, sprigtail, and crow-bill ducks. Patuxent River, per day: 75 rail (ortolan), 75 reedbirds.

---

[1] See Allen *v.* Leighton, 32 Atl., 877 (Maine, 1895); State *v.* Nergaard, 102 N. W., 899 (Wisconsin, 1905).

Massachusetts: One deer; 15 gray squirrels, 15 ruffed grouse, 20 woodcock, 20 quail a season; 5 gray squirrels, 3 ruffed grouse, 4 woodcock, 4 quail, 15 black ducks a day.

Michigan: Two deer, 50 each of partridges, spruce hens, woodcock, plover, 50 in all of snipe and other shore birds a season; 6 in all of partridges and spruce hens a day, 15 in possession; 6 woodcock, 6 plover a day, 20 each in possession; 10 in all of snipe and other shore birds a day, 20 in possession; 25 in all of ducks, geese, and brant a day or in possession at one time.

Minnesota: One deer, 1 moose a season; 15 birds a day; 45 quail, partridges, ruffed grouse, pheasants, prairie chickens, white-breasted or sharp-tailed grouse, doves, plover, woodcock combined; 50 snipe, duck, goose, brant, any aquatic fowl combined, in possession at a time.

Mississippi: One deer a day, 5 a season; 20 each of quail, wild turkeys, robins, cedarbirds, plover, tatlers, chorooks, grosbecs, coots, poule d'eau, rails, ducks, geese, brant, swans a day.

Missouri: One deer, 2 turkeys, 10 of any other species a day; or 2 deer, 4 turkeys, 15 of any other species in possession at a time.

Montana: Three deer (one doe and 2 bucks, or 3 bucks), 1 elk, 1 goat, 1 sheep (male) a season; 5 each of grouse, partridges, prairie chickens, fool hens, pheasants, sage hens, and 20 ducks a day.

Nebraska: Ten squirrels, 10 quail, 10 prairie chickens or grouse, 10 wild geese or brant, and 25 game birds of any other variety a day; 20 squirrels, 10 prairie chickens or grouse, 10 wild geese or brant, or 50 other game birds in possession at one time.

Nevada: Two deer a season; 15 mountain quail, 15 valley quail, 10 sage hens, 6 grouse, 5 plover, and 15 snipe, 20 ducks, 10 geese, 3 swans a day.

New Hampshire: Two deer a season in Coos, Carroll, and Grafton Counties, 1 in rest of State.

New Jersey: One deer a season; 10 rabbits, 10 quail, 3 ruffed grouse, 3 English or ringneck pheasants, 3 Hungarian partridges, 10 woodcock, 30 marsh hens, 20 ducks, 10 each of geese and brant a day or in possession. (Not applicable to dealer in game, hotel keeper, etc., during open season at place of business.)

New Mexico: One deer a season; 4 wild turkeys, 6 grouse, 20 ducks, 30 other birds a day or in possession at one time.

New York: Two deer, 20 woodcock, 20 grouse, 3 male imported pheasants a season; 6 varying hares or rabbits, 5 squirrels, 4 woodcock, 4 grouse, 25 waterfowl (limit for one boat or battery, 40), 15 rails, coots, mudhens or gallinules (limit for one boat 20), 15 shore birds (limit for one boat 25) a day. Long Island: 50 quail, 20 ruffed grouse, 36 male pheasants a season; 10 quail, 4 ruffed grouse, 6 male pheasants, and 6 cottontail or varying hares a day.

North Carolina: Brunswick, New Hanover, Pender, 15 marsh hens a day; Buncombe, 2 deer a season, 25 partridges, pheasants, wild turkeys, or doves a day; Cabarrus, Mecklenburg, Surry, 15 quail (partridges) a day; Cleveland, 10 quail (partridges) a day; Dare, 5 deer a season; Haywood, 1 buck a day, 2 a season; 2 pheasants, 2 wild turkeys, or 20 birds in all, a day; Henderson, Jackson, 2 bucks a season; Madison, 25 birds a day; Transylvania, 3 deer a season, 5 squirrels, 20 quail (partridges) a day.

North Dakota: Ten prairie chickens, grouse, cranes, combined a day, 20 in possession at one time; 25 plover, snipe, woodcock, ducks, geese, brant combined, 50 in possession at one time.

Ohio: Five squirrels, 12 each of plover, snipe, woodcock, shore birds, rail, geese, 25 ducks a day.

Oklahoma: One deer a season; 1 turkey (male) March 15–April 15, 3 turkeys, November 15–January 1; 25 quail, plover, curlew, snipe, other shore birds, or ducks a day, 150 a season; 15 prairie chickens a day, 100 a season; 15 doves a day, 150 a season; 10 geese or brant a day; 1 swan a season.

Oregon: Three deer a season; 5 silver gray squirrels and 10 quail in 7 consecutive days; 5 sage hens a day, 10 in 7 consecutive days in district 2; 5 ruffed grouse, pheasants, sooty or blue grouse, and male Chinese pheasants a day, 10 in 7 consecutive days; 10 doves (State) and wild pigeons (district 1) a day 20 in 7 consecutive days; 30 shore birds, rail, coot, ducks, and geese in 7 consecutive days.

Pennsylvania: One deer a season; 6 squirrels, 10 rabbits or hares a day; 10 quail a day, 40 a week, 75 a season; 5 ruffed grouse a day, 20 a week, 50 a season; 10 each of English, Mongolian, or Chinese pheasants and woodcock a day, 20 a week, 50 a season; 5 Hungarian partridges a day, 20 a week, 30 a season; 1 wild turkey a day, 2 a season. Possession limited to season's limit.

Rhode Island: No limits.

South Carolina: Five deer a season; 25 quail (partridges), 2 wild turkeys, 25 doves, 12 woodcock, a day.

South Dakota: One deer a year; 20 waterfowl, 10 other birds a day; 25 partridges, ruffed grouse, prairie chickens, sharp-tailed (white-breasted) grouse, pheasants, woodcock, golden plover and upland plover, in aggregate in possession at one time; 50 snipe and waterfowl in aggregate in possession at one time.

Tennessee: Fifty ducks; 30 of all other birds in aggregate a day. Lauderdale County; 6 each of squirrels, ducks, and geese a day.

Texas: Three deer a season; 25 birds a day (3 wild turkeys December 1 to March 1).

Utah: One deer (residents only), 25 grouse a season; 15 quail, 8 sage hens, 6 grouse a day or in possession at one time; 12 geese a day, and 25 in all of snipe, ducks, geese a day.

Vermont: One deer and 25 ruffed grouse or woodcock a season; 5 each of rabbits or gray squirrels a day or in possession; 4 each of quail, ruffed grouse, partridges or woodcock a day; 10 in all of plover, English snipe, and other shore birds a day; 20 ducks a day.

Virginia: No limits.

Washington: Two deer (Okanogan County, 1 male), 1 sheep, 1 goat, 1 antelope, 1 caribou, a season; 5 in all of partridges, grouse, prairie chickens, and pheasants, 10 quail a day; 25 upland game birds a week; 20 in all of ducks, geese, and brant a week (week begins at midnight Wednesday night). If the bag of upland game birds includes quail, the limit is 10 a day.

West Virginia: Two deer a season; 12 quail a day, 96 a season; 6 ruffed grouse a day, 25 a season; 2 wild turkeys a day, 6 a season.

Wisconsin: One deer a year; 5 grouse, prairie chickens, woodcock, 10 partridges, 15 plover, snipe, coots, rail, rice hens, ducks, 10 geese or brant, a day; 20 of all kinds of birds in possession by resident in one day.

Wyoming: One deer, 2 elk (resident, 1 female and 1 additional elk under special license), 1 male sheep a season; 18 birds (of which not more than 6 may be grouse) a day, or in possession at one time.

Alberta: One deer, 1 elk, 1 moose, 1 caribou, 2 antelope, 2 sheep, 2 goats a season; 10 grouse, partridges, pheasants, prairie chickens, ptarmigan a day, or 100 a season.

British Columbia: Three deer, 1 elk, 2 moose (1 in county of Kootenay), 3 caribou, 3 goats, 2 sheep (1 in county of Kootenay), 250 ducks and snipe a season. (Nonresident licensee may kill 5 deer, caribou, and goats, but not more than 3 of any one species, and 3 moose, elk, and sheep, but not more than the bag limit of any one species.)

Manitoba: One in all of deer, elk, moose, caribou, and antelope a season; 20 in all of grouse, partridges, prairie chickens a day, 100 a season; 20 ducks a day in September, 50 ducks a day in October and November.

New Brunswick: Two deer, 1 moose, 1 caribou a season (lumber camp limited to 2 moose, 2 caribou a season); 10 partridges, 10 woodcock, 20 ducks a day.

Newfoundland: Three caribou (2 stags and one doe) a season.

Nova Scotia: One moose a season; 5 ruffed grouse, 10 woodcock a day.

Ontario: One deer, 1 moose, 1 caribou a season. Two or more persons hunting together under license may kill an average of 1 deer each; 10 partridges a day.

Prince Edward Island: No limits.

Quebec: Zone 1: Two deer, 1 moose, 2 caribou a season. Zone 2: Two deer, 1 moose, 4 caribou a season; 3 deer and 3 caribou additional may be taken by persons domiciled in Province under $5 permit.

Saskatchewan: Two in all of deer, elk, moose, caribou, and 2 antelope a season; 10 in all of grouse partridges, pheasants, prairie chickens, ptarmigan a day, or 100 a season; 50 waterfowl a day, 250 a season.

Yukon: Six caribou or deer, 2 moose, 2 elk, 2 sheep, 2 goats, 2 musk oxen a season.

LICENSES FOR HUNTING AND SHIPPING GAME.

In Arkansas nonresidents are not permitted to hunt, except on their own premises.[1] In all the States and throughout Canada licenses must be secured before nonresidents can hunt any or certain kinds of game (see fig. 2, p. 51). In 40 States[2] and 7 Canadian Provinces a like restriction is imposed on residents, but the fees are usually much smaller, and often are merely nominal (see fig. 3, p. 51).

A special kind of hunting license, often known as the "alien" license, is being generally adopted to restrict hunting by persons who are not citizens of the country, and is now in force in about half of the States.

In Maine,[3] Wyoming, New Brunswick (on wild lands), and Nova Scotia nonresidents are not permitted to hunt big game unless accompanied by qualified guides.

Landowners or taxpayers are not required to pay the usual fee in a number of States, and no license is required of those hunting in their own county in Michigan and Minnesota (birds), Texas or Nova Scotia. Special exemptions are made in favor of nonresident members of fish and game clubs by Massachusetts, Rhode Island, and Quebec. In Virginia no license is required of bona fide guests of residents, and in Ontario no fee is charged for a guest license.

Details in regard to hunting licenses are given in the table on pages 52–59. In every case the fee includes the amount charged for issuing the license. The term commissioner unless otherwise qualified means the game or fish commissioner.

---

[1] Except in a few counties.

[2] Including Tennessee, which has only an optional license; otherwise 39 States have a general resident license.

[3] On wild lands of the State, except from December 1 to 15.

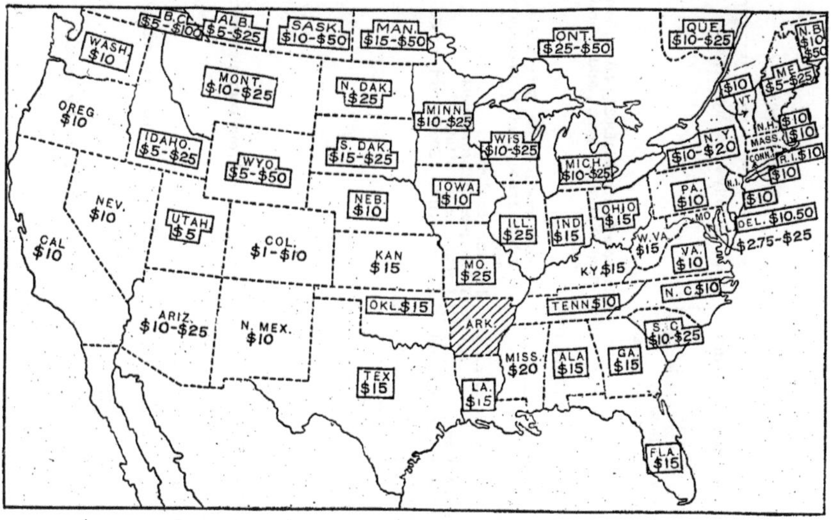

FIG. 2.—States and Provinces which require nonresidents to obtain hunting licenses.

[Inclosed names indicate the States which specifically permit licensees to take a limited amount of game out of the State. Alaska and Newfoundland have $50, Nova Scotia $30 and $15, and Prince Edward Island $15 nonresident licenses, with export privileges. Arkansas does not permit hunting by nonresidents, except in a few counties.]

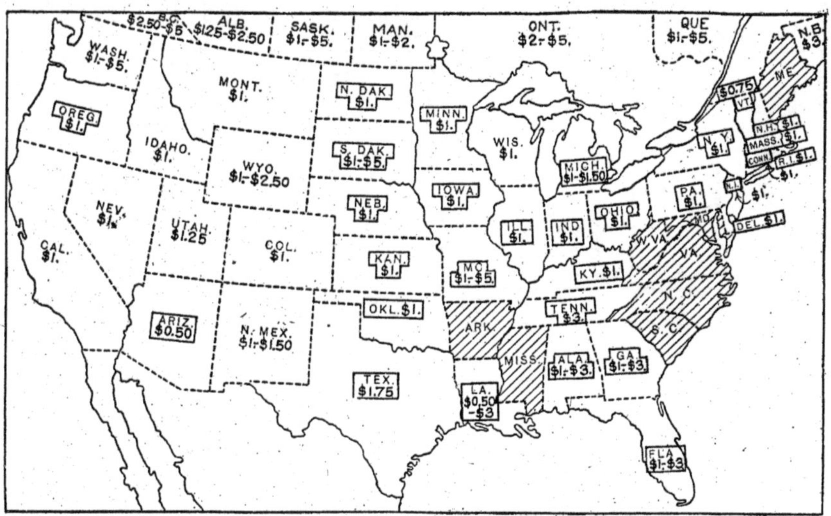

Fig. 3.—States and Provinces which require residents to obtain hunting licenses.

[In Connecticut, Delaware, New Jersey, New York, Ohio, Oklahoma, Pennsylvania, and Rhode Island an additional fee of 10 to 25 cents is charged for issuing the license. Inclosed names indicate States which permit residents to hunt on their own land without license. Nova Scotia and Newfoundland have $5 resident licenses for hunting caribou. Note that many of the States adopt the French method of exempting landowners, while some, particularly in the West, follow the English method of requiring everyone who hunts to obtain a license.]

Details of hunting licenses and export regulations.

State.	Kind of license.	Fee.	By whom issued.	Details of license.	Export limit.
Alabama	Nonresident	$15.00	Probate judge	Not required on lands owned or leased by hunter. Expires Dec. 31.	Game lawfully killed by licensee.
	Alien	15.00	do	do	
	Resident	3.00	do	State license; required outside of county of residence, except on lands owned or leased by hunter.	
	do	1.00	do	County license; not required on lands owned or leased by hunter. Expires Dec. 31.	
Alaska	Nonresident	50.00	Governor	Expires Dec. 31	2 moose (north of lat. 62°), 4 deer, 3 caribou, 3 sheep, 3 goats, and 3 brown bears.
	Alien (nonresident)	100.00	do	do	
	Guide		do	American citizen or native of Alaska. Fee fixed by governor.	
	Shipping (resident)[1]	40.00	do	Export of heads or trophies by resident	1 moose (north of lat. 62°), 4 deer, 2 caribou, 2 sheep, 2 goats, and 2 brown bears.
	do	10.00	do	do	1 caribou or sheep.
	do	5.00	do	do	1 deer, goat, or brown bear.
	Shipping (special)[1]	150.00	do	Export of moose from southern Alaska	1 moose, south of lat. 62°.
Arizona	Nonresident	25.00	Warden or license collector	Deer licenses not required for hunting on own land	Under permit. See Export, p. 38.
	do	10.00	do	Birds	
	Alien	100.00	do	Deer	
	do	25.00	do	Birds	
	Resident [2]	.50	do	General. Duplicate license, 10 cents	
Arkansas				Nonresidents not permitted to hunt [3]	No export.
California	Nonresident	10.00	Fish commissioner, county clerks.	Expires June 30	No export.
	Alien	25.00	do	do	
	Resident	1.00	do	do	
Colorado	N[illegible]ent or alien	10.00	Commissioner or county recorder.	Expires Dec. 31	Permit required from commissioner.
	do	2.00	do	County license for birds, good for 1 week	
	do	1.00	do	County license for birds, good for 1 day	
	do	12.00	do	Hunting and fishing license. Expires Dec. 31	
	Resident	1.00	do	do	
	Guide	5.00	Commissioner	Must also have State hunting license	
Connecticut	Nonresident	10.25	City or borough clerk	Expires Dec. 31	No quail, ruffed grouse, or woodcock.
	Alien	15.25	do	do	
	Resident (citizen)[4]	1.25	do	do	
Delaware	Nonresident	10.50	Commission	Expires Dec. 31	See p. 39.
	Resident	1.10	do	Not required of owners or tenants or their children hunting on their estates. Expires Dec. 31.	
Florida	Nonresident or alien	15.00	County judge	County license	Game lawfully killed by licensee.
	Resident	3.00	do	State license	
	do	1.00	do	County license; not required on own land or in ward of residence.	

Georgia	Nonresident	15.00	Commissioner or county warden.	State license. Expires Feb. 1.	Game lawfully killed.
	Resident	3.00	do	do	
	do	1.00	do	[illegible] license good [illegible] in county of [illegible]; not [illegible] on lands of [illegible]. [illegible] Feb. 1.	
Idaho[5]	Nonresi[illegible] or alien.	25.00	Warden, and deputies	Big [illegible]. [illegible] Mar. [illegible].	2 deer, 1 ibex, 1 mountain goat, 1 mountain sheep, 1 elk. No birds. (See p. 39.)
	[illegible]	5.00	do	Birds only.	
	Resident [illegible]	1.00	do	Hunting [illegible]. Not required of women or [illegible] 12 years old.	
Illinois	N[illegible]	25.50	City or county clerk	[illegible] 1.	Not more than 50 birds of all kinds.
	[illegible]	1.00	do	N[illegible] [illegible] owners and tenants of farms hunting [illegible].	
Indiana	N[illegible]	15.50	Clerk of circuit court	Good [illegible] 1 [illegible].	Nonresident: 15 birds of all kinds, or 45 in case of 3 or more days' consecutive hunting. Resident: No export.
	[illegible][6]	1.00	Commissioner, clerk of circuit court.	Not [illegible] of [illegible] hunting on their own lands, [illegible] of [illegible] or tenants.	
Iowa	N[illegible]	10.50	County auditor	Expires [illegible] 1.	25 of all kinds of game.
	[illegible]	1.00	do	Not [illegible] owners [illegible] of [illegible] lands, or their [illegible], hunting on [illegible].	
Kansas	Nonresident	15.00	Secretary of state	Not [illegible] of [illegible] hunting [illegible] their own [illegible]. [illegible] 30.	No export.
	[illegible]	1.00	County clerk	do	
Kentucky	N[illegible] or alien.	15.00	do	[illegible] Dec. 31.	No quail, grouse, pheasant, wild turkey.
	[illegible]	1.00	do	[illegible] Dec. [illegible]. Not [illegible] of [illegible] [illegible] of [illegible] on [illegible] own [illegible] or [illegible] farms.	
Louisiana	Nonresident or alien.	15.00	Tax collector	Not required [illegible] resident alien hunting on his own [illegible]. Good [illegible].	Nonresident: 1 day's limit of game if not for sale. Resident: No export.
	Market hunting	10.00	do	[illegible]	
	Resident	3.00	do	[illegible]. Not [illegible] of pe[illegible] on [illegible] own [illegible].	
	do	.50	do	[illegible] not [illegible] in [illegible].	

[1] Not more than one general ($40) license and two special ($150) moose licenses issued to one person in one year. Each shipper must file with customs office at port of shipment an affidavit that he has not violated the game law; that the trophy to be shipped has not been bought or purchased, has not been sold, and is not shipped for purpose of sale; that he is the owner of the trophy, and, in case of moose, whether the animal from which it was taken was killed north or south of latitude 62°.

[2] Not required of children under 17 years old if accompanied by holders of general license.

[3] But see State *v.* Mallory, 83 S. W., 955, deciding that nonresidents may hunt on their own land. A few counties make exceptions, and issue local licenses, viz, Bradley, Chicot, Clay, Crittenden, Dallas, Desha, Grant, Hot Spring, Jefferson, Lonoke, Monroe, Phillips, St. Francis, and Stone.

[4] No license is required of a bona fide resident of Connecticut, or his lineal descendants, hunting on land occupied by him and used for agricultural purposes.

[5] Not required of veterans of the Civil War.

[6] Applicant under 14 years old must furnish written consent of parent or guardian.

Details of hunting licenses and export regulations—Continued.

State.	Kind of license.	Fee.	By whom issued.	Details of license.	Export limit.
Maine	Nonresident	$25.00	Commissioners	All game during October, November, and December	Nonresident: 1 moose, 2 deer, 10 each of partridges and woodcock, 15 ducks; also one pair of game birds a month under 50-cent tag.
	do	5.00	do	Game that may be shot before Nov. 1 in certain counties. Holder may obtain big-game license by paying $20 additional.	
	do.[1]	5.00	do		
	Resident alien	15.00	do	Not required of aliens who pay taxes or who have resided in State 2 years continuously prior to application.	
	[illegible]	5.00	do		
	[illegible] (…t).	20.00	[illegible]	Guide to be registered, and to guide not more than 5 persons at a time. Expires Dec. 31.	
	[illegible])	1.00	[illegible]	do	
	[illegible] (…t).		[illegible]	Moose, $5; deer, $2; one pair of game birds in seven days, 50 cents.	
Maryland	N[illegible] [2]	$5.00 25.50	Cl[illegible] court [3]	Separate county laws	Local laws.
Massachusetts [4]	Alien	15.00	[illegible]	Required of unnaturalized foreign-born residents	10 birds of all kinds.
	Nonresident	[5] 10.00	Commissioners	Expires Dec. 31	
	[illegible]	1.00	[illegible]	Not required of persons hunting on land which they own or on which they live.	
Michigan	N[illegible] alien	25.00	[illegible] clerk	Deer	1 deer under permit. 1 day's bag limit of birds.
	[illegible]	10.00	[illegible]	Small game only. Not required of persons hunting on their own lands.	
	[illegible]	1.50	[illegible]	Deer. Good for season	
	[illegible]	1.00	do	Small game. Not required in county of residence or of landowners, their minor children, or employees hunting on own land.	
	Export	10.00	State warden		Nonresident landowner and member of a club maintaining a game preserve may export 20 ducks or migratory birds killed by him on said premises.
Minnesota	Nonresident	25.00	Commissioners	Game animals. Expires Dec. 31	1 deer, 25 birds.
	do	10.00	do	Game birds	
	Resident	1.00	County auditor	Deer and moose. Expires Dec. 31	
	do	1.00	do	Game birds. Not required in county of residence. Expires Dec. 15.	
Mississippi	Nonresident	20.00	Sheriff	County license. Landowners and their nonresident relatives and friends hunting on their lands exempt. Good for season.	No export.
Missouri	Nonresident	25.00	Commissioner	Expires Dec. 31	2 deer, 4 turkeys, 50 of other species.
	Resident	5.00	County clerk or license collector.	State license. Expires Dec. 31	
	do	1.00	do	County license. Required for hunting in county of residence or in adjoining counties. Not required of owners or tenants of farm lands hunting on such lands. Expires Dec. 31.	

Montana	Nonresident	25.00	Warden	Hunting and fishing. Expires Apr. 30	
	do	10.00	do	Hunting and fishing. Birds only	Number permitted to be killed (see p. 49).
	Alien	30.00	do	do	
	Resident [6]	1.00	Warden or justice of peace	do	
	Guide	10.00	Warden	Good for 1 year	
	Shipping	.50	do	Permits limited export in op[illegible] season	
Nebraska	Nonresident	10.00	Commissioner or county clerk.	Hunting and fishing. Expires Dec. 31	50 birds.
	Resident	1.00	do	Hunting and fishing. Not required of boys under 18 accompanied by parents or guardians, or of [illegible]sons hunting on [illegible] lands they own or [illegible].	
Nevada	Nonresident	10.00	[illegible] clerk or warden	Not required of women, of [illegible] under 14, or of persons hunting on their own lands.	No export.
	Alien	25.00	do	Good for 1 year	
	Resident	1.00	do	do	
New Hampshire [7]	Nonresident or alien	10.00	Commissioner	Expires Dec. 31. Not required of landowner (or im[illegible] family) hunting on his own land.	2 deer, 12 birds.
	Resident	1.00	Commissioner and town [illegible].	do	
	Guide	1.00	[illegible]		
	do	20.00	do	Resident. Expires Dec. 31	
New Jersey	Nonresident	10.50	[illegible] clerk	Nonresident. Expires Dec. 31	
				Expires Dec. 31	10 rabbits, 50 reedbirds, 50 rail, and 15 other birds a day.
	Alien	10.50	[illegible], city, or town [illegible].	Not required of [illegible] or lessee of farm land [illegible] on land on [illegible] he resid[illegible].	
	Resident [illegible]	1.15	do	Not required of landowner or members of family [illegible] on his land and hunting thereon.	
New Mexico	Nonresident or alien	10.00	Warden or deputy	Nonresident paying taxes to amount of $100 entitled to a resident license.	
	Resident	1.50	do	General	Under permit.
	do	1.00	do	Big game, including turk[illegible]	
	do	1.00	do	[illegible] [illegible], except turkeys	
	[illegible]	5.00	do		

[1] For [illegible] that may be [illegible] Oct. 1 in Aroostook, [illegible] and Washington [illegible].

[2] County and [illegible] are [illegible] at [illegible]: [illegible], $10.50; Baltimore, [illegible] of State, $5.20, [illegible] of [illegible], $20.20 (rabbit, quail, [illegible]); [illegible], $10.50; Caroline, $5; Carroll, $10.50; Cecil, [illegible] (rabbit, [illegible], grouse, [illegible], reedbird, rail, [illegible] and black, and [illegible]); [illegible], $20.50 (rabbit, quail, and [illegible]; [illegible] of State, [illegible] of county, [illegible], $15.50; Garrett, $25.50; [illegible] except [illegible]); Howard, $8; Kent, $15.50, $5.50 if [illegible] by [illegible] owner (all [illegible] game); [illegible], $15.50; [illegible], $11 ([illegible]); Prince George, $20.50 ([illegible] game); Queen [illegible], $4.50; St. [illegible] (upland game); Somerset, [illegible], $2.75, [illegible], $10.50; [illegible], $10.50 (not [illegible] if [illegible] be secured [illegible] or lessee); [illegible], $10.50; Worcester, [illegible]. Guests of [illegible] no [illegible], except in Allegany, [illegible], Caroline, Cecil, [illegible], Talbot, and [illegible]. [illegible] grants [illegible] if [illegible] of his [illegible].) [illegible] hunting by [illegible] of the [illegible] except by [illegible] and [illegible] by [illegible]. In [illegible] as [illegible]: [illegible], $1.20 (rabbit, squirrel, [illegible]); [illegible], by and brush [illegible] Bay), $5 (South [illegible]), $2.50; [illegible] and Elk [illegible]), [illegible], $5.50 (on [illegible], Elk, and [illegible] Rivers), [illegible], $1; [illegible], [illegible] boat, $5.75, sink box, $20.75; [illegible], $2.50; [illegible], $2.50, sink box, $10.50; [illegible] Flats, [illegible], $5.75, sink box, $20.75; [illegible] Bay, sink box or [illegible].

[3] In [illegible].

[4] [illegible] under 16 [illegible] or [illegible].

[5] [illegible] of [illegible] real [illegible] than [illegible] and [illegible] to 1907, owners or [illegible] 18 years old of real [illegible] than [illegible], or [illegible] than 4 days) [illegible] of [illegible].

[6] [illegible] club [illegible], pay a fee of $1.

[7] Li[illegible] to [illegible] under 18 without written [illegible] of [illegible] or [illegible].

Details of hunting licenses and export regulations—Continued.

State.	Kind of license.	Fee.	By whom issued.	Details of license.	Export limit.
New York	Nonresident or alien.	$20.50	County, city, or town clerk.	Fee for nonresident taxpayer, $10.50. Alteration, transfer, or loan of license a forgery in second degree. Expires Dec. 31.	1 deer, and day's bag limit under shipping license.
	Resident	1.10	do	Alteration of license a forgery. Not required of owner or lessee (or immediate family) occupying and cultivating farm land and hunting on such land.	
North Carolina	Nonresident (Audubon).	10.25	Clerk of superior court	Good only in 37 counties not covered by following and 3 local licenses. Not required of parents and children of landowners hunting on their grounds.	50 partridges or quail, 12 grouse, 2 turkeys, 50 beach birds or snipe.
	Nonresident (special).[1]	10.50	do	Good only in county of issue.	
North Dakota	N[illegible]nt	25.00	County auditor	Expires Dec. 15.	Nonresidents only. 2 deer; 20 (in all) of grouse, prairie chickens, doves, cranes, and swans; 50 (in all) of plover, snipe, ducks, geese, and brant. Resident; no export.
	[illegible]t[2]	1.00	do		
Ohio	[illegible]nt	15.25	Clerk county court or town clerk.	Expires Dec. 5.	25 animals and birds.
	[illegible]nt	1.25	do	Exp[illegible]ies Dec. 31. Not required of landowner, his children, or [illegible]t [illegible]nting on own land.	
Oklahoma	N[illegible]nt	$15.00	Warden or county clerk	[illegible]ies M[illegible]y 1.	2 days' bag limit.
	Alien	25.00	do	do	
	[illegible]t citizen	1.25	do	Not [illegible]d of m[illegible]r [illegible]r 14 years, or [illegible]n [illegible]nting on his [illegible]n or [illegible]d lands.	
Oregon[3]	Nonresident	10.00	County clerk	N[illegible]t [illegible]d of [illegible]er [illegible]d family [illegible]ing on [illegible]n [illegible] [illegible]es. Expires Dec. 31.	No e[illegible]pt [illegible] [illegible]d, except by Wash[illegible] [illegible], who may take 1 [illegible]s bag.
	Alien	25.00	Commission	[illegible]n [illegible]e [illegible]es n[illegible]t [illegible]t [illegible]ing.	
	Resident	1.00	County clerk	[illegible]ing [illegible]d [illegible]ing. Not [illegible]d of [illegible]er [illegible]d family [illegible]ing on [illegible]n [illegible] [illegible]es.	
Pennsylvania	Nonresident	10.00	County treasurer	G[illegible]d f[illegible]r [illegible]r of s[illegible]se. [illegible]s n[illegible]t [illegible]d [illegible]nt.	1 day's bag limit.
	Resident[3]	1.15	County treasurer or justice of the peace.	E[illegible]pies Dec. 31. [illegible] [illegible]n 14 n[illegible]t [illegible]d to [illegible]nt. [illegible]t [illegible]d of [illegible]n landowner, his [illegible]ly, or [illegible]s [illegible]ing on [illegible]nd or [illegible]d [illegible]nt [illegible] [illegible]der p[illegible]mit.	
Rhode Island[3]	Nonresident[4]	10.15	City or town clerk	E[illegible]pies D[illegible]e. 31.	10 birds.
	Alien	15.15	do		
	Resident	1.15	do	Not required of owner or occupant of agricultural land (or immediate family) hunting on such land.	
South Carolina	Nonresident and alien.	10.25	County clerk	All game except quail and turkeys. Good for season.	2 deer, 4 wild turkeys, 12 ruffed grouse, 50 each of partridges (quail), beach birds, ducks, geese.
	do	25.00	do	County license for quail and turkeys. Not required of person hunting on land he owns or controls or guest of and accompanied by resident freeholder.	
	Market hunting	50.00	County treasurer	County license for residents hunting wild fowl on public lands and navigable waters. Expires Dec. 31.	

South Dakota	Nonresident	25.00	W[illegible]n or county treasurer.	Big game and game birds. Expires June 30	Birds lawfully in possession.
	do	15.00	do	Game birds only	
	[illegible]	5.00	County treasurer	County license. Big game. Issued in county in which hunting is to be done.	
	do	1.00	do	Game birds. Not required of landowner hunting on his own land.	
Tennessee	Nonresident	10.25	State [illegible]	Not required of landowner paying $100 taxes. Expires Dec. 31.	Nonresident: 50 ducks; 30 of all other birds in aggregate. Resident: No export.
	Resident	3.00	do	Required when hunting on lands with verbal permission of owner.	
	Market hunting	25.00	do	Annual license; $200 bond required	
Texas	Nonresident	15.00	[illegible]	Expires Dec. 31	3 deer, 75 ducks, 1 day's bag limit of other birds.
	Resident	1.75	County clerk	Not required in county of residence or adjoining counties or on land controlled by hunter. Expires Sept. 1.	
Utah	Nonresident	5.00	Commissioner or justice of peace.	Hunting and fishing. Expires Dec. 31. Not required for rabbits.	Nonresident: 1 day's bag limit. Resident: No export.
	Alien	15.00	do	do	
	Resident	1.25	do	Hunting and fishing. Not required of females or children under 12 or for hunting rabbits.	
Vermont [3]	Nonresident [5]	10.50	Town clerk	Expires July 1	Nonresident: 1 deer; birds as stated on p. 38. Resident: 1 season's bag under license.
	Resident	.75	do	Not required of owners or tenants of farm lands (or their minor children) hunting on such lands.	
Virginia [6]	Nonresident [7]	10.00	County clerk	Good in open season in the 6 months following issue	1 deer, 50 quail, 10 pheasants or grouse, 3 wild turkeys, 25 of each or 100 in all, plover, snipe, sandpipers, willets, curlew, and tatlers.
Washington	Nonresident	10.00	State auditor	State license. Expires Mar. 1	N[illegible] [illegible] or [illegible] [illegible]: A [illegible] [illegible] of [illegible] [illegible] and a [illegible] [illegible] of [illegible]. [illegible]: No [illegible].
	do	5.00	County auditor	County license	
	Alien, nonresident	50.00	State or county auditor	State or county license	
	Alien	15.00	State auditor	[illegible] license. [illegible] certificate required	
	Resident	5.00	do	State license	
	do	1.00	County auditor	County license	
West Virginia	Noncitizen	15.50	County clerk	[illegible]. [illegible] for 1 [illegible] [illegible] [illegible] of [illegible] or [illegible] [illegible] is [illegible] 15.	No [illegible], [illegible], [illegible] grouse, [illegible] [illegible], [illegible] [illegible].

[illegible] in [illegible] [illegible] 58 [illegible]: Beaufort, Bertie, [illegible] [illegible] [illegible], [illegible] [illegible], [illegible], [illegible], [illegible] and [illegible], Dare, Davie, Duplin, F[illegible], [illegible] [illegible], Gates, Graham, [illegible], [illegible], [illegible], [illegible], [illegible], [illegible], [illegible], [illegible], [illegible], [illegible], [illegible], Polk, [illegible], [illegible], [illegible], [illegible], [illegible], [illegible], [illegible], [illegible], [illegible], [illegible], [illegible], [illegible], Washington, Wayne, [illegible], [illegible], Yadkin. Special [illegible] [illegible] are in force in [illegible] [illegible] (also [illegible] export [illegible]), [illegible], [illegible], Transylvania, [illegible], Union, [illegible], [illegible], [illegible], Haywood, Hyde, [illegible], [illegible], Northampton, [illegible], [illegible], Craven, Dare [illegible] ([illegible]), [illegible], [illegible] [illegible], and W[illegible] [illegible]. [illegible] of [illegible] are given in [illegible] No. 30, [illegible] of [illegible] may be had [illegible] on [illegible] [illegible] [illegible] Survey, U. S. [illegible] of [illegible].

[2] Not [illegible] of [illegible] or [illegible] of [illegible] [illegible] or [illegible] of his [illegible] [illegible] [illegible] [illegible] on [illegible] [illegible].

[3] *Oregon:* [illegible] under 14 [illegible] [illegible] not [illegible] to [illegible] with gun except on [illegible] [illegible] or [illegible] [illegible], [illegible], or [illegible]. In [illegible] and *Vermont*, [illegible] under 16 [illegible] [illegible] [illegible] [illegible] of [illegible] or [illegible]. In [illegible], [illegible] must be 15 [illegible].

[4] [illegible] [illegible] and [illegible] of [illegible] or [illegible] [illegible] [illegible] to Jan. 1, [illegible], [illegible] [illegible] to [illegible] [illegible] of [illegible], and [illegible] [illegible] [illegible] [illegible] [illegible] at [illegible] [illegible] [illegible], pay a fee of $1.15.

[5] Fee 75 [illegible] for [illegible] of [illegible] [illegible] in [illegible] [illegible] at [illegible] who pays [illegible] [illegible].

[6] [illegible] [illegible] [illegible] [illegible] [illegible] [illegible] [illegible] [illegible] ([illegible] 4 [illegible]) [illegible] [illegible] [illegible] or [illegible] on [illegible] land.

[7] [illegible] not [illegible] to [illegible] [illegible] to [illegible] [illegible] of [illegible], [illegible] [illegible] [illegible] [illegible] [illegible], [illegible] or [illegible], [illegible] [illegible] [illegible] and [illegible] with him.

Lightning Source UK Ltd.
Milton Keynes UK
UKHW011147051118
331792UK00005B/351/P

9 780266 874157